How this book will help you

by Paul Metcalf

Exam practice – how to answer questions better

This book will help you improve your performance in your GCSE Intermediate or Higher Mathematics exam.

I mark hundreds of exam papers and find that students make the same mistakes on the same questions each year. For this reason, lots of students fail to get the grade that they are capable of achieving.

This book has been written to help you to tackle exam questions correctly so that you can achieve a really high grade. **Students gain high GCSE grades in Mathematics through a combination of** good knowledge, good understanding and good examination technique. **It is the last of these with which this book will particularly help you**.

Each chapter in the book is broken down into four separate elements, aimed at giving you as much guidance **and** practice **as possible:**

1 Exam Questions and Answers

The questions and answers at the start of each chapter are typical of the topic area. **In the 'How to score full marks' section, I show you how to tackle the questions in order to arrive at the correct answers. This means that** when you see questions like this on your exam paper, you will know exactly how to go about answering them in order to score full marks.

2 'Key points to remember'

This section identifies the **key elements** of the topic and the **essential knowledge** you need in order to answer exam questions. I have picked out what I think to be the most important points – but you will also need to use your own notes and textbook.

3 'Don't make these mistakes'

This section highlights common errors and misconceptions. Many of these errors seem quite logical when you are not actually sitting there taking the exam! It is a good idea, when you are into your last minute revision, to read quickly through all of these sections and make doubly sure you avoid these mistakes.

4 Questions to try, Answers and 'How to solve these questions'

Each chapter ends with a set of exam questions which I have carefully chosen as typical of those which you will meet in your exam. Don't cheat. Sit down and try to answer the questions as if you were in the exam. Try to remember all that you've read earlier in the chapter and put it into practice.

The answers are at the back of the book, and they are ones that would gain full marks. **Alongside each answer, I have put comments to help you understand how to solve the question.** This means that if you haven't got the right answer, you can read through what I've written and find out where you went wrong. This will help you get the right answer next time around in your exam.

All about your Maths exam

Written papers and calculators

The majority of GCSE Maths exams are assessed on the basis of **two written** papers. You will be expected to answer one of these papers using a calculator and the other paper without a calculator.

Some of the questions in this book should be answered without the use of a calculator. They have this symbol by them.

Some questions would be very difficult to answer without using a calculator, or specifically need to be answered with the use of a calculator. They have this symbol by them.

In general, though, when you are using this book, it is a good idea to **practise answering questions with and without the use of a calculator**.

Exam Tips

- **Always read the question carefully** and make sure that you answer all of the parts.
- **Always show your working** and write down your calculations.
- **Make sure that your answer is reasonable** and appropriate to the question set.
- **Don't cross out any work** until you have replaced it by something better.
- If you get stuck on a question, then miss it out and **come back to it later on**.
- Make sure you haven't missed out any pages by mistake (especially the back page).
- When you have finished **go back and check through your work again**.
- Recheck your answer to question 1 – this is often answered wrongly the first time.

The topics covered by your specification

The content and assessment of the different Exam Boards' GCSE specifications are very similar and usually differ only in the way in which coursework is assessed.

This book is divided into 23 chapters covering the most common mathematical topics in the GCSE Mathematics specifications:

Shape, Space and Measures	Chapters 1–6
Number	Chapters 7–11
Handling Data	Chapters 12–17
Algebra	Chapters 18–23

I have selected the questions from across all Exam Boards. Have a go at all of them as plenty of practice really will help you to achieve a high grade.

Tiers of entry

All GCSE Maths exams are offered at **three tiers** and the available grades are as follows:

Tier of entry	Available grades
Foundation tier	**D, E, F, G and U only**
Intermediate tier	**B, C, D, E and U only**
Higher tier	**A*, A, B, C and U only**

The written papers assess the full range of grades for the tier of entry. The papers consist of **questions of varying lengths** and you will be expected to answer all of the questions on the paper itself.

Intermediate or Higher?

Some of the chapters in this book are aimed at students sitting Intermediate papers and some at those sitting Higher papers. If you are entered for the Intermediate tier, then you do **not** need to cover the work for the Higher tier which is identified by a large **H** at the top of each page in the chapter.

Exam Questions and Answers

1 The diagram shows three triangles P, Q and R.

(a) Describe fully the single transformation which takes P onto Q.

(b) Describe fully the single transformation which takes P onto R.

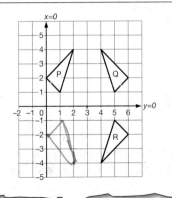

Answer

(a) Reflection in x = 3

(b) Rotation of 180° about the point (3, 0)

How to score full marks

● The single transformation is a reflection.

● You should have noticed that all the coordinates on this line have an *x*-value of 3, so the equation of the line is $x = 3$.

● Here, the single transformation is a rotation.

● The rotation is 180°. You don't need to say clockwise or anticlockwise as the result is the same in either case.

● The centre of rotation is (3, 0); you must state this for full marks.

2 (a) Describe fully the transformation that maps triangle T onto triangle A.

(b) Reflect triangle T in the line *y* = *x* and label the image B.

(c) Rotate triangle T through 90° anticlockwise about (0, 1) and label the image C.

Answer

(a) Reflection in the x-axis (or the line y = 0).

(b) See the diagram opposite.

(c) See the diagram opposite.

How to score full marks

● The transformation is a reflection in the *x*-axis, or you can describe it as the line $y = 0$.

● Both transformations are shown on this diagram.

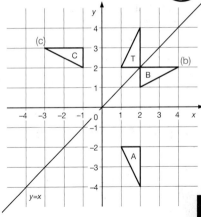

Key points to remember

Object and image

The object is the point or collection of points before the transformation. The image is the point or collection of points after the transformation.

Subsequent images of points ABC ... are usually written as A'B'C'..., A"B"C" ... or else $A_1B_1C_1...$, $A_2B_2C_2...$.

Different transformations

You need to be able to recognise and describe these transformations:

- reflection
- rotation
- enlargement
- translation

Reflection

In a reflection, any two corresponding points on the object and image are the same distance away from a fixed line (called the line of symmetry or mirror line), but on opposite sides of it.

Define a reflection by giving the position of the line of symmetry.

Rotation

In a rotation, lines between any two corresponding points on the object and on the image meet at a fixed point (called the centre of rotation) and they always make the same angle.

Define a rotation by giving the angle (or turn) and direction of the rotation along with the position of the centre of rotation.

Translation

In a translation, the distance and the direction between corresponding points on the object and image are the same.

Define a translation by giving the distance and direction of the translation, usually in the **vector form** $\begin{pmatrix} a \\ b \end{pmatrix}$ where a is the distance in the x-direction and b is the distance in the y-direction.

Enlargement

In an enlargement, the distance between a point on the image and a fixed point (called the **centre of enlargement**) is a factor or multiple of the distance between the corresponding point on the object and the fixed point.

Define an enlargement by giving the scale factor and the position of the centre of enlargement.

$$\text{scale factor} = \frac{\text{distance of point on image from centre}}{\text{distance of corresponding point on object from centre}}$$

or

$$\text{scale factor} = \frac{\text{distance between two points on the image}}{\text{distance between two corresponding points on the object}}$$

Don't make these mistakes ...

Combinations of transformations

Don't forget that two or more transformations can usually be combined as a single transformation. If the question asks for the single transformation then you must identify one transformation and describe it fully.

Describe it fully means:

Transformation	Provide information on:
Reflection	line of reflection
Rotation	angle + direction + centre of rotation
Enlargement	scale factor + centre of enlargement
Translation	units across and units up (usually as a vector)

Q1

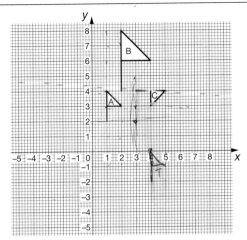

(a) Draw the image of the flag A after a translation of $\begin{pmatrix} -4 \\ 3 \end{pmatrix}$. Label it T.

(b) Describe fully the single transformation that will map:

    (i) A onto B   (ii) A onto C.

Q2 (a) Reflect the triangle ABC in the y-axis. Label the reflection A'B'C'.

(b) Reflect the triangle A'B'C' in the line $y = x$. Label the reflection A"B"C".

(c) Describe fully the single transformation which maps the triangle A"B"C" back onto ABC.

Q3

Parallelogram A is drawn on the grid above.

(a) Enlarge A with centre of enlargement C and scale factor 2.

(b) (i) Calculate the area of A.   12 cm²

    (ii) Calculate the area of the enlarged parallelogram.   48 units²

    (iii) What is the ratio of these areas in the form 1 : n?   1 = 4

Q4 An enlargement scale factor $\frac{1}{4}$ and centre (0, 0) transforms parallelogram ABCD onto $A_1B_1C_1D_1$. The parallelogram $A_1B_1C_1D_1$ is translated by vector $\begin{pmatrix} 3 \\ -2 \end{pmatrix}$ onto $A_2B_2C_2D_2$. What are the coordinates of the points A_2, B_2, C_2 and D_2?

$A_2 = 2,0$

$B_2 = 0,0$

$C_2 = 4,-3$

$D_2 = 0,-3$

Q5

(a) Rotate the rectangle P through an angle of 90° clockwise about centre of rotation (0, 0). Label the rotation Q.

(b) Rotate the rectangle Q through an angle of 90° anticlockwise about centre of rotation (3, 2). Label the rotation R.

(c) Describe fully the single transformation which maps the rectangle P onto R. $\begin{pmatrix} 5 \\ 2 \end{pmatrix}$

The answers are given on pages 89–90.

2 Pythagoras' theorem

Exam Questions and Answers

1 The dimensions of the rectangle are shown in the diagram.
Calculate the length of the diagonal. Leave your answer in surd form.

Diagram not to scale

5 cm

10 cm

Answer

$x^2 = 5^2 + 10^2$
$x^2 = 25 + 100$
$x^2 = 125$
$x = \sqrt{125}$
Diagonal = $\sqrt{125}$ cm

How to score full marks

- Start by drawing a diagram with the diagonal identified.

x

5 cm

10 cm

- Use Pythagoras' theorem to find the length of the hypotenuse (diagonal).

- Square the numbers and remember
  $5^2 = 5 \times 5 = 25$ (not 10)
  $10^2 = 10 \times 10 = 100$ (not 20).

- Take the square root on both sides to find the length.

- Leave your answer as a surd (i.e. as a square root). You could simplify $\sqrt{125}$ to get $\sqrt{125} = \sqrt{5 \times 5 \times 5} = 5\sqrt{5}$.

Note: On a calculator paper you may be asked to give your answer to an appropriate degree of accuracy (say 3 significant figures).

Your answer will look like this.

$x^2 = 125$
$x = \sqrt{125}$
$x = 11.180\,339\,887\,5$
$x = 11.2$ (3 s.f.)
Diagonal = 11.2 cm (3 s.f.)

2   An oil rig is 15 kilometres east and 12 kilometres north from Kirrin.
   (a) Calculate the direct distance from Kirrin to the oil rig.
       (The distance is marked x on the diagram.)
   (b) An engineer flew 14 kilometres from Faxtown to the oil rig.
       The oil rig is 10 kilometres west of Faxtown.
       Calculate how far south the oil rig is from Faxtown.
       (The distance is marked y on the diagram.)

Not drawn accurately

Answer

(a) $x^2 = 12^2 + 15^2$
     $x^2 = 144 + 225$
     $x^2 = 369$
     $x = \sqrt{369}$
     $x = 19.209\,373$
     $x = 19.2$ km (1 d.p.)

(b) $14^2 = y^2 + 10^2$
        $196 = y^2 + 100$
     $196 - 100 = y^2$
        $96 = y^2$
         $y^2 = 96$
          $y = \sqrt{96}$
          $y = 9.797\,959\,0$
          $y = 9.8$ km (1 d.p.)

How to score full marks

- You should start by using Pythagoras' theorem to find the length of the hypotenuse (marked x).

- Square the numbers you know, add them and then take the square root of both sides.

- Round the answer to a suitable degree of accuracy and remember to include the units of distance.

- The second part of the question uses Pythagoras' theorem, but take care as the length (marked y) is **not** the hypotenuse. This sort of question is popular on exam papers!

- Subtract 100 from both sides to isolate the y^2 term, then simplify.

- Place the y^2 on the left-hand side (to make y^2 the subject).

- Take the square root of both sides.

- Round the answer to a suitable degree of accuracy and remember to include the units of distance.

Right-angled triangles

For any right-angled triangle, the square of the length of the hypotenuse is equal to the sum of the squares of the lengths on the other two sides.

$$c^2 = a^2 + b^2$$

For a right-angled triangle, the side opposite the right angle is called the hypotenuse and this is always the longest side.

If you are given the hypotenuse, use $c^2 = a^2 + b^2$

If you are not given the hypotenuse, use $c^2 = a^2 + b^2$ and rearrange as:

$$a^2 = c^2 - b^2 \quad \text{or} \quad b^2 = c^2 - a^2$$

Pythagorean triples

The set of numbers:

3, 4, 5 is called a Pythagorean triple because $3^2 + 4^2 = 5^2$
5, 12, 13 is called a Pythagorean triple because $5^2 + 12^2 = 13^2$

Pythagorean triples are **sets of three whole numbers** that satisfy the rule for Pythagoras' theorem.

If you know your Pythagorean triples then you can solve right-angled triangles easily …

Remember 3, 4, 5 and 5, 12, 13… and also any multiples of them:

3, 4, 5
6, 8, 10   are all this shape:
9, 12, 15 …

5, 12, 13
10, 24, 26   are all this shape:
15, 36, 39 …

Don't make these mistakes ...

Remember that **calculate** means you **must calculate** the answer, so **don't just measure** it from the diagram.

This is particularly true where the diagram has any of the following notes written next to it:

Diagram not drawn to scale
*Diagram **not** accurately drawn*
Not to scale
Not drawn to scale
Not drawn accurately

Remember that x^2 means $x \times x$ (it does **not** mean $x \times 2$).
So, for example, $3^2 = 3 \times 3$, $4^2 = 4 \times 4$, $5^2 = 5 \times 5$, $6^2 = 6 \times 6$ … although 2^2 is equal to 2×2 which (presumably) causes the problems!

Remember that on a non-calculator paper you may need to leave your answer in surd form – but check you can't simplify – $\sqrt{25} = 5$, $\sqrt{121} = 11$.

Careful!

These numbers do **not** form a Pythagorean triple.

Q1 The diagram on the right shows the layout of five paths in the garden.

AB is 8.3 m long. BC is 6.1 m long. BD is 5.0 m long. ABC and BDA are both right angles.

(a) Calculate the length of the path AC, giving you answer to a suitable degree of accuracy. *10.3. (1dp)* ✓

(b) Calculate the length of the path AD, giving you answer to a suitable degree of accuracy. *6.62 (2dp)* ✓

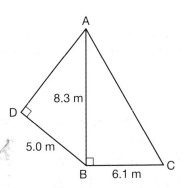

Q2 Calculate the length of a diagonal of a square of side 10 cm. Leave your answer in surd form.

√25+25
√50
Ans: 2√50 ✗
√200

Q3 Calculate the height of this isosceles triangle. Leave your answer in surd form.

√10²−4²
= √100−16
= √84

Q4 This is a parallelogram. The lengths marked are in centimetres.

(a) Work out the area of the parallelogram. State the units of your answer. *4×2=8cm²* *5×4 = 20cm²* *Ans= 20cm²* ✓

(b) Work out the perimeter of the parallelogram. State the units of your answer. *√2²+4² = √16+4 = √20 = 4.5 (1dp)* *4.5 +4.5+7 +7 =23cm* ✓

Not to scale

Q5 A ladder, 2.75 m long, leans against a wall.

The bottom of the ladder is 1.80 m from the wall, on level ground.

Calculate how far the ladder reaches up the wall.

Give your answer to an appropriate degree of accuracy. *Ans: 2.07m (3dp)*

√2.75²+1.8² ✗
= 3.287 (3dp)
= 3.3 (1dp)

√2.75²−1.8²

Not drawn to scale

Q6 The triangle ABC has vertices at A(3, −1), B(6, 1) and C(−1, 5). Find the lengths AB, BC and CA and prove that ABC is a right-angled triangle.

8units
7units
4units

3 Angle and tangent properties of circles

Exam Questions and Answers

---

1 In the diagram, O is the centre of the circle.
Angle COA = 100°.
Calculate: (a) angle CBA (b) angle CDA.

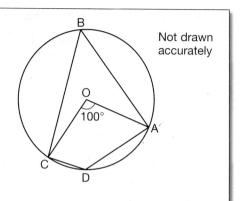

Not drawn accurately

Answer

(a) angle CBA = 50°

(b) angle CDA = 130°

How to score full marks

- ∠CBA = 50° (as the angle subtended by an arc AC at the centre is twice that subtended at the circumference)

- ∠CDA = 130° (as the opposite angles of a cyclic quadrilateral ABCD are supplementary so they add up to 180°)

---

2 A, B, C and D are four points on the circumference of a circle centre O.
AT is a straight line passing through the centre of the circle.
The tangent PT meets the circle at D.
Given that OÂD = 25°, find **each** of the following angles.
Give reasons for your answer.
(a) AB̂C (b) CÔD
(c) AD̂T (d) CD̂T

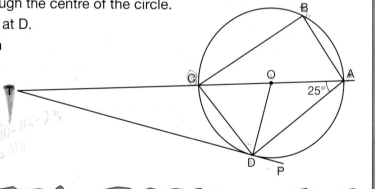

Answer

(a) AB̂C = 90°

(b) CÔD = 50°

(c) AD̂T = 115°

(d) CD̂T = 25°

How to score full marks

- AB̂C = 90° (as the angle in a semicircle is always 90°)

- CÔD = 50° (as the angle subtended by an arc/chord CD at the centre, CÔD, is twice that subtended at the circumference, CÂD)

- AD̂O = 25° (base angles of isosceles triangle ODA)

- OD̂T = 90° (tangent is perpendicular to the radius)

- AD̂T = AD̂O + OD̂T = 25° + 90° = 115°

- CD̂T = 25° (as the angle between a tangent and a chord equals the angle subtended by the chord in the alternate segment)

Key points to remember

Properties of angles in circles

- The angle subtended by an arc (or chord) at the centre is twice that subtended at the circumference.

$$y = 2x$$

- The angle in a semicircle is always 90°.

$$a = 90°$$

- Angles subtended by the same arc (or chord) are equal.

$$p = q = r$$

- The opposite angles of a cyclic quadrilateral are supplementary (they add up to 180°).

$$a + c = 180°$$
$$b + d = 180°$$

Properties of chords in circles

- A perpendicular from the centre of a circle to a chord bisects the chord.

r is the radius of the circle

$$AC = CB$$

Conversely, a perpendicular bisector of a chord passes through the centre of the circle.

- Chords that are equal in length are equidistant from the centre of the circle.

If AB = PQ then $x = y$

Conversely, chords that are equidistant from the centre of a circle are equal in length.

Properties of tangents to circles

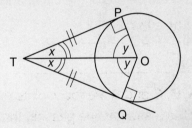

- A tangent to a circle is perpendicular to the radius at the point of contact.
- Triangles TPO and TQO are similar:
  ∠TPO = ∠TQO
  ∠POT = ∠QOT
  TP = TQ
  PO = QO (radii of circle)
- Tangents to a circle from an external point are equal in length.

Don't make these mistakes ...

For these questions you should always use the properties given to find the angles – don't measure, especially where the diagram has a note to say that it is not drawn to scale.

Never presume the values of angles, always look for evidence ... the angle may look like a right angle but how can you be sure?

Don't forget that the radius of a circle is always the same length, so watch out for isosceles triangles.

You will be required to give a 'proof' of your answers ... so learn the properties given above.

Q1

O is the centre and AB is a diameter of the circle.

OD is parallel to BC and angle BAC = 56°.

Calculate the size of:

(a) angle ABC   34

(b) angle AOD   34   ✓

(c) angle ACD   17   ✓

(d) angle OAD.   ~~73~~ 73 ✓

The tangents to the circle at B and C meet at T.

Calculate the size of:

(e) angle BOT.

56 ✓

90+56=146

180-146=34

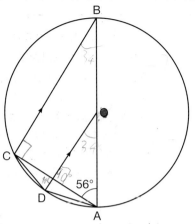

Diagram not drawn accurately

Q2

PQ and PR are tangents to a circle. Their points of contact are Q and R respectively.

O is the centre of the circle and angle POR = 75°.

Find:

(a) ∠POQ   75°   ✓

(b) ∠OPQ   15°   ✓

(c) ∠OPR.   15°   ✓

180 - 75 = 90 ✓
= 15°

Not to scale

Q3

AB, BC and CA are tangents to the circle at P, Q and R respectively.

The centre of the circle is at O.

AC is parallel to PO and angle ACB is 40°.

Work out angle POQ.

130° ✓

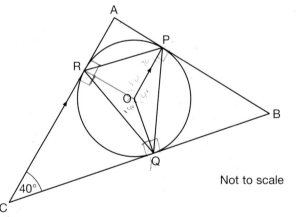

Not to scale

Q4

A chord AB is drawn on a circle of radius 6 cm. If the perpendicular distance of the chord from the centre of the circle is 4 cm, calculate the length of the chord.

$2\sqrt{20}$

$\sqrt{4^2+6^2}$

Q5

Two chords PQ and RS are parallel to each other, on opposite sides of a circle of radius 15 cm. If PQ = 10 cm and RS = 12 cm, find the distance between the chords.

10 cm

27.9 (1dp)

12 cm

The answers are given on pages 92–94.

4 Sine, cosine, tangent

Exam Questions and Answers

1 The diagram shows a vertical pole, AB, standing on horizontal ground DBC.

The pole is held by two wires AC and AD.

The wire AC is 16 m long and makes an angle of 54° with the ground.

(a) Calculate the length of the pole AB. Give your answer to an appropriate degree of accuracy.

(b) The distance CD is 25 m. Calculate the angle the wire AD makes with the ground.

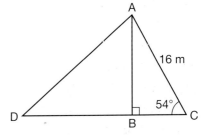

Diagram not drawn to scale

Answer

(a) $\sin 54° = \dfrac{opp}{hyp}$

$\sin 54° = \dfrac{AB}{16}$

$AB = 16 \times \sin 54°$

$AB = 12.944\,271\,91$

$AB = 12.9 \text{ m (3 s.f.)}$

(b) $\cos 54° = \dfrac{adj}{hyp}$

$\cos 54° = \dfrac{BC}{16}$

$BC = 16 \times \cos 54°$

$BC = 9.404\,564\,037$

$BD = DC - BC$

$BD = 25 - 9.404\,564\,037$

$BD = 15.595\,435\,96$

$\tan \theta = \dfrac{AB}{BD}$

$\tan \theta = \dfrac{12.944\,271\,91}{15.595\,435\,96}$

$\tan \theta = 0.830\,003\,851$

$\theta = 39.692\,803\,8\ldots°$

$\theta = 39.7° \text{ (3 s.f.)}$

How to score full marks

- The identified sides are 'opposite' and 'hypotenuse' so use:

$$\text{sine } x = \frac{\text{opposite}}{\text{hypotenuse}}$$

- Rearrange the equation to make AB the subject.

- Round to an appropriate degree of accuracy (3 s.f. or 1 d.p. seems appropriate here).

Diagram not drawn to scale

- To calculate the angle ADB you need to know more about the triangle ADB. You have found that AB = 12.944 271 91 m

- You know that DC = 25 m but to find BD you need to work out BC first…

- The identified sides are 'adjacent' and 'hypotenuse' so use:

$$\text{cosine } x = \frac{\text{adjacent}}{\text{hypotenuse}}$$

- Now to find ∠ ADB, the identified sides are 'adjacent' and 'opposite' so use:

$$\text{tangent } x = \frac{\text{opposite}}{\text{adjacent}}$$

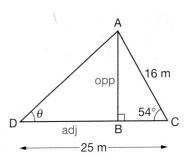

- Having found the value of tan θ, you can now use a calculator to find $\tan^{-1} 0.830\,003\,851$ (or arctan 0.830 003 851) to find the value of θ.

- Round the answer to an appropriate degree of accuracy.

2 The diagram shows the position of two radio masts, A and B.

B is 4 km south and 6 km east of A.

Calculate the bearing of B from A.

Not to scale

Answer

$\tan x = \frac{4}{6}$

$x = \tan^{-1} \frac{4}{6}$

$x = 33.690\,068°$

The bearing $= 270° + 33.690\,068°$
$= 303.690\,068°$
$= 304°$ (to the nearest degree)

How to score full marks

● To find the bearing you first need to find the angle marked x on the diagram.

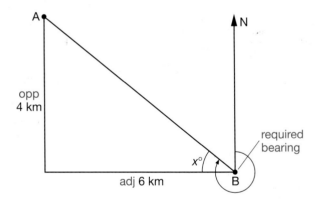

● The identified sides are 'adjacent' and 'opposite' so use:

$$\text{tangent } x = \frac{\text{opposite}}{\text{adjacent}}$$

● Now you can use your calculator to find $\tan^{-1} \frac{4}{6}$ (or $\arctan \frac{4}{6}$) to find the angle.

● Finally, round to an appropriate degree of accuracy.

The sides of a right-angled triangle are given special names, as in the diagrams.

Of course the adjacent side and the opposite side depend on which angle you are considering, so it is important to label the sides you know and the sides you want to know.

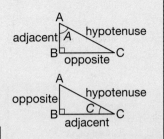

Sine of an angle

The sine of an angle (abbreviated as sin)

$$= \frac{\text{length of opposite side}}{\text{length of hypotenuse}}$$

So $\sin A = \dfrac{\text{length of opposite side}}{\text{length of hypotenuse}} = \dfrac{BC}{AC}$

and $\sin C = \dfrac{\text{length of opposite side}}{\text{length of hypotenuse}} = \dfrac{AB}{AC}$

Tangent of an angle

The tangent of an angle (abbreviated as tan)

$$= \frac{\text{length of opposite side}}{\text{length of adjacent side}}$$

So $\tan A = \dfrac{\text{length of opposite side}}{\text{length of adjacent side}} = \dfrac{BC}{AB}$

and $\tan C = \dfrac{\text{length of opposite side}}{\text{length of adjacent side}} = \dfrac{AB}{BC}$

Cosine of an angle

The cosine of an angle (abbreviated as cos)

$$= \frac{\text{length of adjacent side}}{\text{length of hypotenuse}}$$

So $\cos A = \dfrac{\text{length of adjacent side}}{\text{length of hypotenuse}} = \dfrac{AB}{AC}$

and $\cos C = \dfrac{\text{length of adjacent side}}{\text{length of hypotenuse}} = \dfrac{BC}{AC}$

Finding angles

You can reverse the process to find the angle, given two sides of a right-angled triangle.

If you are given the lengths of the sides, use the following ratios to find the angles.

$\sin^{-1} \dfrac{\text{opposite}}{\text{hypotenuse}}$ or arcsin $\dfrac{\text{opposite}}{\text{hypotenuse}}$

$\cos^{-1} \dfrac{\text{adjacent}}{\text{hypotenuse}}$ or arccos $\dfrac{\text{adjacent}}{\text{hypotenuse}}$

$\tan^{-1} \dfrac{\text{opposite}}{\text{adjacent}}$ or arctan $\dfrac{\text{opposite}}{\text{adjacent}}$

Angles are frequently represented by Greek letters of the alphabet such as $\alpha, \beta, \gamma, \delta, \theta, \phi$ ....

Angles of elevation and depression

The angle of elevation is the angle up from the horizontal.

The angle of depression is the angle down from the horizontal.

Don't make these mistakes ...

Most important!
Don't forget to check that:
- your calculator is set to DEG (degree) mode
- you are dealing with a right-angled triangle.

Don't muddle 'adjacent' and 'opposite'. Identify the angle you are using and then label the opposite and adjacent sides (these will depend upon the identified angle).

For an acute angle (an angle between 0° and 90°):

the sine and the cosine of the angle are always less than 1.

If your answer is not between 0 and 1, it is wrong!

Always check that your answers are reasonable:
- the longest side is always opposite the right angle
- the smallest side is opposite the smallest angle.

Remember that the angles of a triangle add up to 180°, so don't waste time using sine, cosine and tangent to find the third angle.

Q1 In the diagram ABCD is a parallelogram.

BC = 5 cm and CD = 10 cm. Angle BCD = 48°.

Given that: sin 48° = 0.7431   *37.2° (1dp)*
            cos 48° = 0.6691
            tan 48° = 1.1106

calculate the area of the parallelogram, giving your answer to an appropriate degree of accuracy.

Q2 A rectangle measures 11 cm by 6 cm.

What angle does the diagonal make with the longest side?

28.6°

Q3 A ship sails a distance of 25 km from a point P, on a bearing of 085°. Calculate how far the ship is:

(a) to the north of P   *21.8 km*

(b) to the east of P.   *24.9 km*

Q4 The diagram shows the positions of three telephone masts A, B and C.

Mast C is 5 kilometres due east of Mast B.

Mast A is due north of Mast B and 8 kilometres from Mast C.

(a) Calculate the distance of A from B.   *0.24 km*
    Give your answer in kilometres, to three significant figures.

(b) (i)   Calculate the size of the angle marked x°.   *x=51.3° (1dp)*
          Give your angle correct to one decimal place.
    (ii) Calculate the bearing of A from C.   *321.3° is the bearing*
          Give your bearing correct to one decimal place.
    (iii) Calculate the bearing of C from A.   *141.3°*
          Give your bearing correct to one decimal place.

Q5 A boat B is moored 40 m from the foot of a vertical cliff. The angle of depression of the boat from the top of the cliff is 42°.

(a) Calculate the height of the cliff.   *36m high*

(b) The boat is released from its mooring and it drifts 250 m directly away from the cliff.   *7.08°*

    Calculate the angle of elevation of the top of the cliff from the boat.

Diagram not drawn to scale

Cliff

7.08°

B

40 m

The answers are given on pages 94–95.

Exam Questions and Answers

1 Find the size of angle A and the area of the triangle.

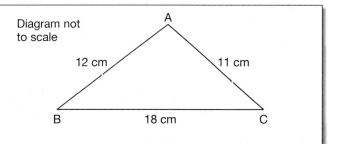

Diagram not to scale

A

12 cm   11 cm

B   18 cm   C

Answer

$$\cos A = \frac{b^2 + c^2 - a^2}{2bc}$$

$$\cos A = \frac{11^2 + 12^2 - 18^2}{2 \times 11 \times 12}$$

$$\cos A = \frac{121 + 144 - 324}{264}$$

$$\cos A = \frac{-59}{264}$$

$\cos A = -0.223\,484\,848$
$A = 102.913\,797\,8°$
$A = 102.9°$ (1 d.p.)

$\text{Area} = \frac{1}{2} ab \sin C$

$= \frac{1}{2} \times 11 \times 12 \times$
$\quad \sin 102.913\,797\,8°$

$= 64.330\,688\,63$
$= 64.3\,\text{cm}^2$ (1 d.p.)

How to score full marks

- You are given three sides and need to find an angle, so you need to use the cosine rule.

$$\cos A = \frac{b^2 + c^2 - a^2}{2bc}$$

- Substitute the given lengths, using the diagram to identify them.

- The negative value tells you that angle A is obtuse.

- Use the inverse button ($\cos^{-1}$ or arccos) on your calculator to find the angle.

- Round the answer to an appropriate degree of accuracy (usually 3 s.f. or 1 d.p.).

- To find the area of the triangle use:

$$\text{area of a triangle} = \frac{1}{2} ab \sin C$$

- Remember to use the most accurate value of A (**not** the rounded value, as this is less accurate).

- Round to an appropriate degree of accuracy (3 s.f. or 1 d.p.).

---

2 Find the size of angle A in this triangle.

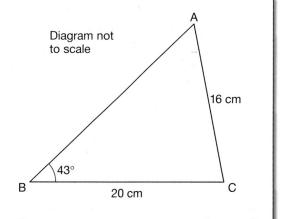

Diagram not to scale

A

16 cm

43°

B   20 cm   C

Answer

$$\frac{\sin A}{20} = \frac{\sin 43°}{16}$$

$$\sin A = \frac{20 \times \sin 43°}{16}$$

$$\sin A = 0.852\,497\,95$$

$A = 58.484\,408\,63°$ or
$A = 121.515\,591\,4°$
$A = 58.5°$ or $121.5°$ (1 d.p.)

How to score full marks

- In this case, since the information involves two sides and two angles then it is appropriate to use the sine rule so:

$$\frac{a}{\sin A} = \frac{b}{\sin B}$$

or $\dfrac{\sin A}{a} = \dfrac{\sin B}{b}$ by reciprocating both sides

- Multiply both sides by 20 to find an expression for sin A.

- Use the inverse button (sin⁻¹ or arcsin) on your calculator.

- Don't forget that the value of $A = 58.484\,408\,63°$ is not unique. The graph shows that there is another possible value which satisfies sin $A = 0.852\,497\,95$.

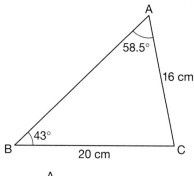

- The other value is $A = 121.515\,591\,4°$ (from the calculator).

- You don't have this problem when you use the cosine rule as a negative value suggests an obtuse angle. When you use the sine rule, you can avoid it by finding the smallest angles first (if possible).

Key points to remember

Cosine rule

$$a^2 = b^2 + c^2 - 2bc\cos A$$

$$\text{or } \cos A = \frac{b^2 + c^2 - a^2}{2bc}$$

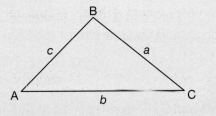

Sine rule

$$\frac{a}{\sin A} = \frac{b}{\sin B} = \frac{c}{\sin C}$$

$$\text{or } \frac{\sin A}{a} = \frac{\sin B}{b} = \frac{\sin C}{c}$$

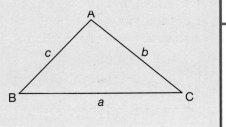

When to use the rules

- Use the cosine rule when you are working with three sides and one angle.
- Use the sine rule when you are working with two sides and two angles.

Area of a triangle

The sine and cosine rules can be extended to find the area of a triangle so that:

$$\text{area of a triangle} = \tfrac{1}{2}ab\sin C$$

where the angle C is the 'included' angle between sides a and b.

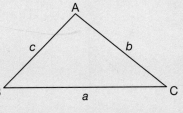

Similarly:

$$\text{area of triangle} = \tfrac{1}{2}bc\sin A$$

$$\text{or area of triangle} = \tfrac{1}{2}ac\sin B$$

Don't make these mistakes ...

When you are using the cosine rule, be careful when you are subtracting $2bc\cos A$. Work it out separately or use brackets:

$$a^2 = b^2 + c^2 - (2bc\cos A)$$

If the cosine of the angle is negative, the angle is obtuse (check that it is opposite the longest side).

If the sine of the angle is negative you have probably made a mistake!

When you are using the sine rule, don't forget that the largest angle might be obtuse. If one of the answers gives θ, the other answer is $180° - \theta$.

Don't use the cosine rule or the sine rule for right-angled triangles.

Questions to try

Q1 The sides of a triangle are 1.5 cm, 2.5 cm and 3.5 cm respectively. Show that the triangle is an obtuse-angled triangle and find the size of the largest angle.

$A \rightarrow$ obtuse angle $A = 120°$ ✓

Q2 The diagram shows triangle ABC.
AB = 8.6 cm, BC = 3.1 cm and
AC = 9.7 cm.

Calculate the angle ABC.

102° ✓

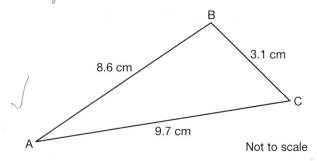

8.6 cm

3.1 cm

9.7 cm

Not to scale

Q3 A ship leaves port and sails on a bearing of 032° for 12 km. The ship then changes direction and sets sail on a bearing of 058° for 15 km.

What is the distance and bearing of the ship from the port?

27 Km   47° ✓ ✓

Q4 A ship, A, is 9.2 km from a port, P, on a bearing of N37°E (037°). Another ship, B, is 4.5 km from P on a bearing of S63°E (117°).

(a) Calculate the distance, AB, between the two ships.

9.51 Km ✓

(b) Calculate the bearing of A from ship B. Give your answer to the nearest degree.

9° ✓

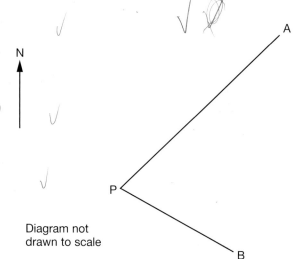

N

A

P

B

Diagram not drawn to scale

Q5 In triangle ABC the length of AB is 8.3 cm and angle ABC is 20°.

D is a point on BC such that the length of DC is 6.1 cm and angle ADB is 105°.

Calculate the length of AC.

6.05 cm ✓

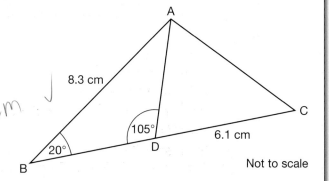

A

8.3 cm

105°

20°

B

D

6.1 cm

C

Not to scale

The answers are given on pages 96–98.

Exam Questions and Answers

1   The diagram shows a trapezium ABCD. AB is parallel to DC and is twice its length.

Given that **AB** = **p** and **DA** = **q**, express each of these vectors in terms of **p** and **q**.

(a) **AC**   (b) **CB**

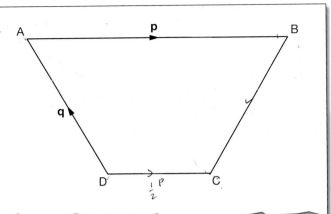

Answer

(a) $\vec{AC} = \frac{1}{2}p - q$

(b) $\vec{CB} = \frac{1}{2}p + q$

How to score full marks

- **AC** = **AD** + **DC**

  $\quad = -\mathbf{q} + \frac{1}{2}\mathbf{AB}$ (as AB is twice the length of DC)

  $\quad = -\mathbf{q} + \frac{1}{2}\mathbf{p}$

  $\quad = \frac{1}{2}\mathbf{p} - \mathbf{q}$

- The last line is not essential, but it looks tidier.

- **CB** = **CD** + **DA** + **AB**

  $\quad = -\frac{1}{2}\mathbf{p} + \mathbf{q} + \mathbf{p}$

  $\quad = \frac{1}{2}\mathbf{p} + \mathbf{q}$

- This answer uses the fact that **CD** = –**DC**. If the letters of a vector are reversed, the vector is acting in the opposite direction. This can often be useful when solving questions like this.

2   In triangle AOB, $\vec{OA}$ = **a** and $\vec{OB}$ = **b**.
X is a point on OA such that OX : XA = 3 : 1.
Y is a point on AB such that AY : YB = 3 : 1.

(a) Express:
    (i) $\vec{OX}$ in terms of **a**
    (ii) $\vec{AY}$ in terms of **a** and **b**
    (iii) $\vec{XY}$ in terms of **a** and **b**.

(b) The line XY is extended to a point P so that YP = $\frac{1}{2}$XY.

    (i)   Express $\vec{BP}$ in terms of **a** and **b**.
    (ii)   Explain why O, B and P are in a straight line.

Not to scale

Answer	How to score full marks

Answer

(a) (i) $\overrightarrow{OX} = \frac{3}{4}\underline{a}$

(ii) $\overrightarrow{AY} = \frac{3}{4}(\underline{b} - \underline{a})$

(iii) $\overrightarrow{XY} = \frac{3}{4}\underline{b} - \frac{1}{2}\underline{a}$

(b) (i) $\overrightarrow{BP} = \frac{1}{8}\underline{b}$

(ii) Since $\overrightarrow{OB} = \underline{b}$ and $\overrightarrow{BP} = \frac{1}{8}\underline{b}$ then the vectors are parallel. Therefore the lines OB and BP are parallel so that O, B and P must lie on a straight line.

How to score full marks

- $\overrightarrow{OX} = \frac{3}{4}\overrightarrow{OA}$ (the line OA is divided into 3 + 1 parts)

  $= \frac{3}{4}\mathbf{a}$

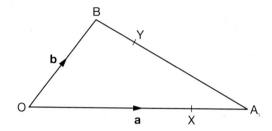

- $\overrightarrow{AY} = \frac{3}{4}\overrightarrow{AB}$ (the line AB is divided into 3 + 1 parts)

  $= \frac{3}{4}(\overrightarrow{AO} + \overrightarrow{OB})$

  $= \frac{3}{4}(-\mathbf{a} + \mathbf{b})$

  $= \frac{3}{4}(\mathbf{b} - \mathbf{a})$

- $\overrightarrow{XY} = \overrightarrow{XA} + \overrightarrow{AY}$

  $= \frac{1}{4}\mathbf{a} + \frac{3}{4}(\mathbf{b} - \mathbf{a})$ (using results from (a)(ii))

  $= \frac{1}{4}\mathbf{a} + \frac{3}{4}\mathbf{b} - \frac{3}{4}\mathbf{a}$

  $= \frac{3}{4}\mathbf{b} - \frac{1}{2}\mathbf{a}$ (tidying up the expression)

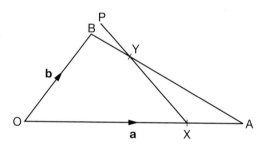

- $\overrightarrow{BP} = \overrightarrow{BY} + \overrightarrow{YP}$

  $= \frac{1}{4}\overrightarrow{BA} + \frac{1}{2}\overrightarrow{XY}$

  $= \frac{1}{4}(-\mathbf{b} + \mathbf{a}) + \frac{1}{2}(\frac{3}{4}\mathbf{b} - \frac{1}{2}\mathbf{a})$

  $= -\frac{1}{4}\mathbf{b} + \frac{1}{4}\mathbf{a} + \frac{3}{8}\mathbf{b} - \frac{1}{4}\mathbf{a}$

  $= \frac{1}{8}\mathbf{b}$

Showing vectors

Vectors can be represented in a number of ways such as:

PQ or you can write $\overrightarrow{PQ}$

r or you can write $\underline{r}$

or as a column vector $\begin{pmatrix} s \\ t \end{pmatrix}$

This form is also used to represent translations, which are vectors since they act in a particular direction.

Equal vectors

Two vectors are equal if they have the same magnitude and direction – i.e. they are the same length and they are parallel.

Addition and subtraction of vectors

To add or subtract vectors, place them end to end with the arrows 'following on' in the same direction.

Components of a vector

The components of a vector are usually described in terms of:

(i) the number of units in the x-direction
(ii) the number of units in the y-direction

These units are best expressed as a column vector.

$$a = \begin{pmatrix} a_x \\ a_y \end{pmatrix}$$

Multiplication of a vector

Vectors cannot be multiplied by other vectors but they can be multiplied by a constant (sometimes called scalar multiplication).

Magnitude of a vector

The magnitude (length) of a vector can be found by using Pythagoras' theorem.

$$|\overrightarrow{AB}| = \sqrt{x^2 + y^2}$$

The length of the vector $\overrightarrow{AB} = \sqrt{x^2 + y^2}$.

You can write $|\overrightarrow{AB}| = \sqrt{x^2 + y^2}$ where the two vertical lines stand for 'magnitude' or length.

Don't make these mistakes ...

Remember that the direction of a vector is important so always show it with an arrow.

If a line is divided in the ratio $x : y$ then there are $x + y$ parts.

The respective fractions are $\dfrac{x}{x + y}$ and $\dfrac{y}{x + y}$.

Q1 Given that $\mathbf{p} = \begin{pmatrix} 5 \\ 4 \end{pmatrix}$ and $\mathbf{q} = \begin{pmatrix} 2 \\ -3 \end{pmatrix}$ estimate these.

(a) $\mathbf{p} + \mathbf{q}$ (b) $2\mathbf{p} - 3\mathbf{q}$ (c) $|\mathbf{p} + \mathbf{q}|$

Q2 PQRS is a trapezium with PQ parallel to SR.

PQRT is a parallelogram.

TR is twice the length of ST.

Given that $\mathbf{QR} = \mathbf{a}$ and $\mathbf{PQ} = \mathbf{b}$, express each of the following in terms of $\mathbf{a}$ and $\mathbf{b}$.

(a) **PT** (b) **PR**

(c) **RT** (d) **SR**

(e) **PS**

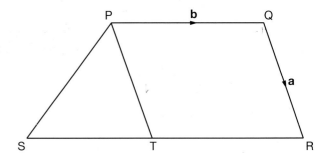

Diagram not drawn to scale

Q3 Vector $\mathbf{a}$, vector $\mathbf{b}$ and the point X are shown on this grid.

(a) Vector $\vec{XY} = 3\mathbf{a} + 1\frac{1}{2}\mathbf{b}$ and vector $\vec{XZ} = 2\mathbf{a} - \frac{1}{2}\mathbf{b}$.

Mark Y and Z on the diagram.

(b) P is the midpoint of YZ.

Express $\vec{XP}$ in terms of $\mathbf{a}$ and $\mathbf{b}$.

You **must** show all your working.

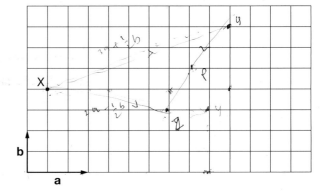

Q4 X and Y are the midpoints of PQ and PR respectively in the triangle PQR. Given that $\vec{XP} = \mathbf{a}$ and $\vec{PY} = \mathbf{b}$ show that QR = 2XY and QR is parallel to XY.

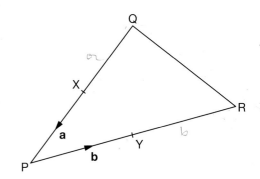

Q5 For the regular hexagon ABCDEF with centre O, $\vec{AB} = \mathbf{a}$ and $\vec{BC} = \mathbf{b}$.

Find: (a) $\vec{AC}$ (b) $\vec{AO}$ (c) $\vec{OB}$ (d) $\vec{AD}$.

What can you say about the quadrilateral ACDF?

Give reasons for your answer.

The answers are given on pages 98–99.

7 Indices and standard form

Exam Questions and Answers

1 The distance from the Earth to the Sun is 9.3×10^7 miles.
Write this number in ordinary form.

Answer

$9.3 \times 10^7 = 9.3 \times 10 \times 10 \times 10 \times 10$
$\times 10 \times 10 \times 10$

$= 93\,000\,000$ miles

How to score full marks

- Remember that $10^7 = 10 \times 10 \times 10 \times 10 \times 10 \times 10 \times 10$.
- Finally, remember to check that your answer is reasonable – and don't forget to include the units.

2 A rectangular picture measures 1.2×10^2 cm by 4.3×10^3 cm.
(a) What is the perimeter of the picture?
(b) What is the area of the picture?
Give your answers in standard form. Remember to state the units in your answers.

Answer

Perimeter
$= 1.2 \times 10^2 + 4.3 \times 10^3$
$+ 1.2 \times 10^2 + 4.3 \times 10^3$
$= 120 + 4300 + 120 + 4300$
$= 8840$
$= 8.840 \times 10^3$ cm

Area
$= (1.2 \times 10^2) \times (4.3 \times 10^3)$
$= 1.2 \times 4.3 \times 10^2 \times 10^3$
$= 5.16 \times 10^{2+3}$
$= 5.16 \times 10^5$ cm^2

How to score full marks

- Remember that the perimeter of a shape is the distance all around it.
- When the power of 10 is the same in two numbers written in standard form, you can just add the decimal numbers together (i.e. $1.2 \times 10^2 + 1.2 \times 10^2 = 2.4 \times 10^2$ and $4.3 \times 10^3 + 4.3 \times 10^3 = 8.6 \times 10^3$) but otherwise you need to convert the numbers to ordinary form.

perimeter $= l + b + l + b$
$= 2l + 2b$

- The question says, 'Give your answers in standard form' so you will lose valuable marks if you don't.
- The question also says, 'Remember to state the units in your answers', so you must do this, too. It is good practice anyway!
- Remember that to find the area of a rectangle you multiply the length by the breadth (or width).

area $= l \times b$

- You should be able to multiply 1.2×4.3 without using a calculator (good practice for the non-calculator paper).
- You should be able to use the rules of indices to show that $10^2 \times 10^3 = 10^{2+3} = 10^5$.
- As the answer is already in standard form, you just need to include the units of area (cm^2) to gain full marks.

27

Key points to remember

You will need to recognise squares and cubes as well as work out square roots and cube roots.

Square numbers are made from other numbers that have been multiplied by themselves, e.g.
1, 4, 9, 16, 25, 36, ...

Cube numbers are made from other numbers that have been multiplied by themselves then multiplied by themselves again, e.g.
1, 8, 27, 64, 125, 216, ...

The square root of a number is the number that is squared to give that number, e.g. the square root of 36 is 6 (because $6 \times 6 = 36$).

The sign $^2\sqrt{}$ or $\sqrt{}$ is used to denote the square root, so $\sqrt{36} = 6$.

The cube root of a number such as 27 is the number that is cubed to give that number, e.g. the cube root of 27 is 3 (because $3 \times 3 \times 3 = 27$).

The sign $^3\sqrt{}$ is used to denote the cube root so $\sqrt[3]{27} = 3$.

You need to remember the rules of indices.

$a^m \times a^n = a^{m+n}$
so $3^7 \times 3^{12} = 3^{7+12} = 3^{19}$

$a^m \div a^n = a^{m-n}$
so $11^6 \div 11^2 = 11^{6-2} = 11^4$

$a^{-m} = \dfrac{1}{a^m}$ so $4^{-2} = \dfrac{1}{4^2} = \dfrac{1}{16}$

Don't forget them just because you are in an exam!

$a^0 = 1$

$a^1 = a$

Questions on standard form can appear on either the calculator or the non-calculator paper. On the calculator paper, you use the $\boxed{EXP}$ or $\boxed{EE}$ keys to input numbers in standard form.

When using your calculator, you must remember to interpret the display – of course, this will depend on your calculator.

$\boxed{3.62\ ^{07}}$ means 3.62×10^7

$\boxed{4.01\ ^{-03}}$ means 4.01×10^{-3}

Don't make these mistakes ...

Don't multiply the number by the power.
Keep reminding yourself that:
$2^5 = 2 \times 2 \times 2 \times 2 \times 2 = 32$
$5^2 = 5 \times 5 = 25$

These are wrong:
$2^5 = 10$ ✗
$5^2 = 10$ ✗

Remember that 2^5 is bigger than 5^2.

Check that your answers are reasonable – remember that a positive power suggests a large number
(e.g. $2.15 \times 10^6 = 2\,150\,000$)
and a negative power suggests a small number
(e.g. $2.001 \times 10^{-5} = 0.000\,020\,01$).

Q1 Work out 6×2^4.

 Q2 Complete this table where each entry is found by adding the numbers in the respective row and column.

+	1^2	2^2	3^2	4^2	5^2	6^2
1^2						
2^2						
3^2						
4^2						
5^2						
6^2						

 Q3 Find, in standard form, the value of each of the following.

(i) $(3.42 \times 10^4) \times (5.91 \times 10^{-11})$

(ii) $\dfrac{4.69 \times 10^{-6}}{7.45 \times 10^4}$

 Q4 If $p = 6 \times 10^{-2}$ and $q = 3 \times 10^{-4}$, calculate the value of:

(a) pq giving your answer in standard form

(b) $p - q$.

 Q5 Light travels at an average speed of 2.998×10^8 m/s.

The distance from the sun to the Earth is approximately 1.496×10^{11} m.

How long will it take light to travel from the sun to the Earth?

Give your answer to the nearest minute.

The answers are given on page 100.

8 Percentages

1   An investment valued at £3500 increases by 8% in one year. What is the new value of the investment?

Answer

1% of £3500 = £35
8% of £3500 = 8 × £35
              = £280

New value = £3500 + £280
            = £3780

How to score full marks

- To find 8% of £3500 you find:
   1% of £3500 = £35
   so 8% of £3500 = 8 × £35 = £280
- The new value of the investment is = £3500 + £280 = £3780
- Or use the fact that after an 8% increase, the new amount
   = 100% of the original amount + 8% of the original amount
   = 108% of the original amount
- The new value of the investment is 108% of £3500.
   1% of £3500 = £35
   108% of £3500 = 108 × £35 = £3780 (as before)

2   The value of a picture is given as £127 200 after a 6% increase. What was the original value of the picture?

Answer

106% of value = £127 200

1% of value = $\dfrac{£127\,200}{106}$

             = £1200

100% of value = 100 × £1200
                 = £120 000

How to score full marks

- £127 200 is 106% of the original value (100% + 6%).
- So 106% of the original value = £127 200
   1% of the original value $= \dfrac{£127\,200}{106}$ (÷ 106)
              = £1200
-    100% of the original value = 100 × £1200   (× 100)
                       = £120 000

A big problem with percentage questions is that they can appear in so many different forms:

- express as a percentage
- find a percentage of a quantity
- find one number as a percentage of another
- calculate a percentage change
- use of percentages (e.g. simple or compound interest)
- reverse percentages

so make sure you know how to tackle each form.

Percentage change

To work out the percentage change, work out the increase or decrease first, then add it to or subtract it from the original amount.

$$\text{percentage change} = \frac{\text{change}}{\text{original amount}} \times 100$$

where the change might be an increase, a decrease, a profit, a loss, an error, ...

Use multipliers ...

If you are really sure you know what you are doing, you can use multipliers for percentage increase or percentage decrease questions, e.g.

- **an increase of 12% means**
  $100\% + 12\% = 112\%$ or $\frac{112}{100} = 1.12$

If the price of an article costing £340 is increased by 12% then the new price is $1.12 \times £340 = £380.80$.

- **a decrease of 8% means**
  $100\% - 8\% = 92\%$ or $\frac{92}{100} = 0.92$

If the price of an article costing £170 is decreased by 8% then the new price is $0.92 \times £170 = £156.40$.

VAT in your head

To find VAT you can use the fact that $17\frac{1}{2}\% = 10\% + 5\% + 2\frac{1}{2}\%$.

First, calculate 10% (divide by 10 to find 10%).

Then calculate 5% (which is half of 10%).

Then calculate $2\frac{1}{2}\%$ (which is half of 5%).

Then add these amounts $(10\% + 5\% + 2\frac{1}{2}\% = 17\frac{1}{2}\%)$ which is easy (even without a calculator).

Don't make these mistakes ...

Don't just divide by 100 when you are asked to find a percentage – make sure you know how to do it.

Don't forget how to find one number as a percentage of another. For example, 30 as a percentage of 40 is $\frac{30}{40} \times 100 = 75\%$.

Don't be put off by reverse percentages, where you are given the amount after the increase (or decrease). Always check your answer by working backwards.

Q1 Find which of $\frac{5}{9}$, 0.7 and 63% is the least and which is the greatest.
You must show all your working.

Q2 The cash price of the saxophone is £740.
Tom buys the saxophone using a credit plan.
He pays a deposit of 5% of the cash price and 12 monthly payments of £65.
Work out the difference between the cost when he used the credit plan and the cash price.

Saxophone

£740 for cash

Credit plan available

Q3 The highest percentage of people unemployed in Great Britain was in 1933.
Out of 13 million people available for work, 3 million were unemployed.
What percentage were unemployed? Give your answer to nearest whole number.

Q4 The population of a town increases by 14% each year. If the population is 35 000 this year then what will it be after:
(a) one year (b) two years?

Q5 The weight of a child is recorded as 25 kg when his actual weight is 25.005 kg.
What is the percentage error on the actual weight?

Q6 A television is advertised at £550 after a price reduction of 12%. What was the original price of the television?

The answers are given on page 101.

9 Rational and irrational numbers

Exam Questions and Answers

1   (a)   Which of the following numbers are rational?

$$1 + \sqrt{2} \qquad \pi^2 \qquad 3^0 + 3^{-1} + 3^{-2}$$

       (b)   When p and q are two different irrational numbers, $p \times q$ can be rational. Write down one example to show this.

Answer

(a) $1 + \sqrt{2}$ irrational

      π^2 irrational

      $3^0 + 3^{-1} + 3^{-2}$

      $= 1 + \frac{1}{3} + \frac{1}{9}$

      $= \frac{13}{9}$ so it is rational

(b) $\sqrt{2} \times \sqrt{8} = 4$

How to score full marks

- Remember that adding or subtracting a rational number and an irrational number always gives an irrational number.
- Remember that any multiple (or power) of π is always irrational.
- There are many examples to illustrate part (b):

> The numbers must be different.

> They must be irrational.

> They must form the square root of a square number.
> e.g. $\sqrt{1} \times \sqrt{1} = 1$ ✗ $\sqrt{3} \times \sqrt{3} = 3$ ✗
> $\sqrt{1} \times \sqrt{4} = 2$ ✗ $\sqrt{1} \times \sqrt{16} = 4$ ✗
> $\sqrt{2} \times \sqrt{2} = 2$ ✗ $\sqrt{2} \times \sqrt{8} = 4$ ✓
> $\sqrt{1} \times \sqrt{9} = 3$ ✗ $\sqrt{4} \times \sqrt{4} = 4$ ✗

> You could also have
> $\sqrt{3} \times \sqrt{12} = 6$
> $\sqrt{5} \times \sqrt{20} = 10$
> $\sqrt{6} \times \sqrt{24} = 12 \dots$
> can you find
> some others?

---

2 $p = 2 + \sqrt{3} \qquad q = 2 - \sqrt{3}$

       (a)   (i)   Work out $p - q$.

            (ii)   State whether $p - q$ is rational or irrational.

       (b)   (i)   Work out pq.

            (ii)   State whether pq is rational or irrational.

Answer

(a) (i) $p - q = 2\sqrt{3}$

     (ii) $p - q$ is irrational

(b) (i) $pq = 1$

     (ii) pq is rational

How to score full marks

- $p - q = 2 + \sqrt{3} - (2 - \sqrt{3})$
         $= 2 + \sqrt{3} - 2 + \sqrt{3}$ Be careful with minus
         $= 2\sqrt{3}$ signs outside brackets.
- $2\sqrt{3}$ includes a surd, so it is irrational.
- $pq = (2 + \sqrt{3})(2 - \sqrt{3})$
         $= 4 - 2\sqrt{3} + 2\sqrt{3} - 3$ Remember FOIL.
         $= 1$

Key points to remember

A rational number can be expressed in the form $\frac{p}{q}$ where p and q are integers.

Examples of rational numbers include $\frac{1}{5}$, $0.\dot{3}$, 7, $\sqrt{9}$, $\sqrt[3]{64}$.

Examples of irrational numbers include $\sqrt{2}$, $\sqrt{3}$, $\sqrt[3]{20}$, π.
Add some of your own examples here.

Rational	Irrational

Irrational numbers involving square roots are also called surds.

Surds can be multiplied and divided.

Remember the rules – there are only two, so it is quite simple!

$$\sqrt{a} \times \sqrt{b} = \sqrt{a \times b} \qquad \frac{\sqrt{a}}{\sqrt{b}} = \sqrt{\frac{a}{b}}$$

Try to recognise the following surds. They often come up on exam papers.

	1 ×	2 ×	3 ×	4 ×	5 ×	6 ×
All of these are multiples of $\sqrt{2}$	$\sqrt{2}$	$\sqrt{8}$	$\sqrt{18}$	$\sqrt{32}$	$\sqrt{50}$	$\sqrt{72}$
All of these are multiples of $\sqrt{3}$	$\sqrt{3}$	$\sqrt{12}$	$\sqrt{27}$	$\sqrt{48}$	$\sqrt{75}$	...
All of these are multiples of $\sqrt{5}$	$\sqrt{5}$	$\sqrt{20}$	$\sqrt{45}$	$\sqrt{80}$	...	
All of these are multiples of $\sqrt{7}$	$\sqrt{7}$	$\sqrt{28}$	$\sqrt{63}$	...		

Don't make these mistakes ...

Don't be misled:
$0.\dot{3}$ looks irrational but
$0.\dot{3} = \frac{1}{3}$ so it is rational.

Don't be put off by repeated numbers.
All recurring decimals are rational –
take my word for it (or ask your
teacher to show you why).

Questions to try

Q1 (a) Write down a rational number x such that $\sqrt{42} < x < \sqrt{44}$.

(b) Write down an irrational number y such that $6 < y < 7$.

(c) Write down a rational number for which the decimal form is never ending.

Q2 Simplify the following.

(a) $\sqrt{98}$

(b) $\sqrt{5} + \sqrt{45}$

(c) $\sqrt{6} \times \sqrt{12}$

Q3 Write $\dfrac{\sqrt{5}}{\sqrt{2}}$ in the form $\dfrac{\sqrt{a}}{b}$
where a and b are whole numbers.

Q4 A rational number, R, is given by the formula $R = (3 - \sqrt{2})^2 + x$.
Calculate a possible value of x.

Q5 (a) $(3 - \sqrt{5}) \times (4 + \sqrt{5}) = a - \sqrt{5}$
Calculate the value of a.

(b) $(3 - \sqrt{5}) \times (4 + \sqrt{5}) + b$ is a rational number.
Give a possible value of b.

Q6 Given that $p = \sqrt{5}$, $q = \sqrt{10}$ and $r = \sqrt{8}$, simplify each of the following, indicating in each case whether your answer is rational or irrational.

(a) $pq - 1$

(b) $\dfrac{q}{pr}$

(c) $(p + q)^2$

The answers are given on page 102.

HIGHER TIER
H

Exam Questions and Answers

1 Convert $0.1\dot{5}$ to a fraction.

Answer

Let $0.1\dot{5} = x$.

Then $10x = 1.5555555 \ldots$

and $1x = 0.1555555 \ldots$

so $9x = 1.4$

$$x = \frac{1.4}{9} = \frac{14}{90} = \frac{7}{45}$$

How to score full marks

- This type of question is easy when you know how to do it. Keep practising these questions and you will soon get the hang of it.

- Notice that:
  $10 \times (\text{fraction}) = 1.5555555\ldots$ (multiplying by 10)
  and $1 \times (\text{fraction}) = 0.1555555\ldots$

- So subtracting gives:
  $9 \times (\text{fraction}) = 1.4$ $(1.5555555\ldots - 0.15555555\ldots)$
  and $(\text{fraction}) = \frac{1.4}{9}$ (dividing both sides by 9)

  but $\frac{1.4}{9}$ is not a proper fraction, so using equivalent fractions:

  $$\frac{1.4}{9} = \frac{14}{90} = \frac{7}{45}$$ (cancelling $\frac{14}{90}$ to its lowest form)

  so $0.1\dot{5} = \frac{7}{45}$

- You can check by putting $\frac{7}{45}$ $(7 \div 45)$ into your calculator.

2 Convert $5.1\dot{5}$ to a fraction.

Answer

$5.1\dot{5} = 5 + 0.1\dot{5}$

Let $0.1\dot{5} = x$.

Then $10x = 1.555 \ldots$

and $1x = 0.1555 \ldots$

So $9x = 1.4$

$$x = \frac{1.4}{9} = \frac{14}{90} = \frac{7}{45}$$

So $5.1\dot{5} = 5 + \frac{7}{45}$

$= 5\frac{7}{45}$

How to score full marks

- Use the same method as above to convert $0.1\dot{5}$ to a fraction, then add the integer (whole number) part to it.

- $5.1\dot{5} = 5 + 0.1\dot{5} = 5\frac{7}{45}$

Common recurring decimals

$\frac{1}{3}$ = 0.333333333333...   you write 0.$\dot{3}$

$\frac{1}{6}$ = 0.166666666666...   you write 0.16$\dot{6}$

$\frac{1}{7}$ = 0.142857142857...   you write 0.$\dot{1}$4285$\dot{7}$

$\frac{1}{9}$ = 0.111111111111...   you write 0.$\dot{1}$

$\frac{1}{11}$ = 0.090909090909...   you write 0.0$\dot{9}$

$\frac{1}{12}$ = 0.083333333333...   you write 0.08$\dot{3}$

Note: All recurring decimals are rational numbers and can be converted to fractions.

Multiplying by 10, 100, 1000, ...

Change 0.$\dot{7}$ to a fraction.

Notice that   10 × (fraction) = 7.77777777777...   (× 10)

and   1 × (fraction) = 0.77777777777...

Subtracting: 9 × (fraction) = 7

and   (fraction) = $\frac{7}{9}$ (dividing both sides by 9)

so 0.$\dot{7}$ = $\frac{7}{9}$

Change 0.$\dot{5}\dot{6}$ to a fraction.

Notice that: 100 × (fraction) = 56.5656565656...   (× 100)

and   1 × (fraction) =   0.5656565656...

Subtracting   99 × (fraction) = 56

and   (fraction) = $\frac{56}{99}$ (dividing both sides by 99)

so 0.$\dot{5}\dot{6}$ = $\frac{56}{99}$

Change 0.$\dot{4}1\dot{3}$ to a fraction.

Notice that: 1000 × (fraction) = 413.413413413...   (× 1000)

and   1 × (fraction) =   0.413413413...

Subtracting   999 × (fraction) = 413

and   (fraction) = $\frac{413}{999}$ (dividing both sides by 999)

so 0.$\dot{4}1\dot{3}$ = $\frac{413}{999}$

In general terms:

$0.\dot{a} = \frac{a}{9}$

$0.\dot{a}\dot{b} = \frac{ab}{99}$

$0.\dot{a}b\dot{c} = \frac{abc}{999}$

where *a*, *b* and *c* are digits of the fraction.

If you remember this, then all you have to do is remember to cancel the fraction to its lowest terms.

Other recurring decimals

Look carefully to see which digits are repeating, then use the same sort of method as above.

Don't make these mistakes ...

Be careful where you put those dots.

0.1$\dot{5}$ = 0.15555 ...

0.$\dot{1}\dot{5}$ = 0.151515 ...

Sometimes a whole group of digits is repeated.

$\frac{1}{7}$ = 0.$\dot{1}$42857$\dot{7}$

Q1 (a) Write the number $0.\dot{4}$ as a fraction in its simplest form.

(b) Write the number $0.\dot{5}$ as a fraction in its simplest form.

How do you think $0.\dot{7}$ and $0.\dot{8}$ can be written as fractions?

Q2 Write the number $0.2\dot{1}$ as a fraction in its simplest form.

Q3 Show that $0.\dot{2}3\dot{4}$ is a rational number.

Q4 Convert $201.\dot{3}\dot{2}$ to a mixed number.

Q5 By considering $\frac{1}{9}$ as a decimal, write $0.7\dot{1}$ as a fraction in its lowest form.

The answers are given on page 103.

Exam Questions and Answers

1 A rectangle measures 12 cm by 7 cm, where each measurement is given to the nearest cm. Write down an interval approximation for the area of a rectangle.

Answer

Minimum area = 11.5 × 6.5
  = 74.75 cm^2

Maximum area = 12.5 × 7.5
  = 93.75 cm^2

Interval approximation
  = 74.75 cm^2 to 93.75 cm^2

How to score full marks

- The minimum values for the two lengths are 11.5 cm and 6.5 cm (as the original lengths are given to the nearest cm).
- The lower bound (minimum area) is found by multiplying the minimum values of the two lengths.
- The maximum values for the two lengths are 12.5 cm and 7.5 cm (as the original lengths are given to the nearest cm).
- The upper bound (maximum area) is found by multiplying the maximum values of the two lengths.

2 A formula used in science is:

$$a = \frac{v - u}{t}$$

The quantities v, u and t are each measured correct to the nearest 0.1.
  $u = 17.4$, $v = 30.3$ and $t = 2.6$.
Find the maximum possible value of a. You must show full details of your calculations.

Answer

Maximum value of

$$a = \frac{30.35 - 17.35}{2.55}$$

  = 5.098 039 216

$a = 5.1$ (to 1 d.p.)

How to score full marks

- It will help if you work out the minimum and maximum values of u, v and t before going any further.

  $u_{min} = 17.35$ $v_{min} = 30.25$ $t_{min} = 2.55$
  $u_{max} = 17.45$ $v_{max} = 30.35$ $t_{max} = 2.65$

- Remember that to get the maximum value of the fraction $\frac{p}{t}$ you need to work out $\frac{p_{max}}{t_{min}}$.
  You need the maximum value of p (p_{max}) for the numerator (top line of the fraction), so work out $v_{max} - u_{min}$.

  You also need the minimum value of t (t_{min}) for the denominator (the bottom line of the fraction), which is 2.55.

- So, for the maximum value of a, work out:

$$a = \frac{v_{max} - u_{min}}{t_{min}} = \frac{30.35 - 17.35}{2.55}$$

  to give $a = 5.098\ 039\ 216$ or $a = 5.1$ to 1 d.p.

- It is best to round your answer to 1 d.p. as the numbers given in the question are given correct to the nearest 0.1.

Key points to remember

Rounding ...

Most measures are rounded. For questions on this topic you need to know how to round:

- to the nearest thousand
- to the nearest whole number
- to the nearest 0.1... .

... and boundaries

If a number is rounded to the nearest thousand, then the boundaries (upper and lower limits) are given by:

number $\pm \frac{1000}{2}$ (i.e. 'number − 500' to 'number + 500')

So if 5000 is given to the nearest 1000 then the boundaries are given by:

$5000 \pm \frac{1000}{2}$

which gives a lower bound of 5000 − 500 or 4500,
    and an upper bound of 5000 + 500 or 5500.

Similarly a number rounded to the nearest whole number will have boundaries given by:

number $\pm \frac{1}{2}$ (i.e. 'number − $\frac{1}{2}$' to 'number + $\frac{1}{2}$')

and a number rounded to the nearest 0.1 will have boundaries given by:

number $\pm \frac{0.1}{2}$ (i.e. 'number − $\frac{0.1}{2}$' to 'number + $\frac{0.1}{2}$').

Finally, you need to remember that:

To find the **maximum value of p − q** you need to work out $p_{max} - q_{min}$ and to find the **minimum value of p − q** you need to work out $p_{min} - q_{max}$.

To get the **maximum value of p ÷ q** you need to work out $p_{max} \div q_{min}$ and to get the **minimum value of p ÷ q** you need to work out $p_{min} \div q_{max}$.

Remember that common sense and constant checking are very good tools for these questions.

Don't make these mistakes ...

Don't apply this method to upper and lower bounds for ages.

If a person's age is 21, it doesn't mean that it ranges from $20\frac{1}{2}$ to $21\frac{1}{2}$.

For an age of 21 the lower bound is 21.
For an age of 21 the upper bound is 22 (actually 21 years, 364 days, 23 hours, 59 minutes and 59 seconds, i.e. a split second before their 22nd birthday, except in a leap year ...).

Q1 For each of the following write down the lower and upper bound.

(a) 5000 (to the nearest thousand)

(b) 5000 (to the nearest 100)

(c) 3.62 (correct to 2 decimal places)

(d) 240 (correct to 2 significant figures)

(e) $7\frac{1}{2}$ (to the nearest half)

Q2 The River Nile is 6695 km long, measured to the nearest kilometre.
What is the shortest possible length, in metres?

Q3 A box measures 12 cm by 9 cm by 10 cm, each to the nearest centimetre.
Find the lower bound and the upper bound for the volume of the box.

Q4 The numbers of people attending two events are given as 8500 and 6300, both
figures being given to the nearest 100. What is the greatest possible difference
in the numbers of people attending these events?

Q5 Assume the Earth to be a sphere of diameter 12 750 km, correct to the nearest 50 km.
Land covers 29% of the Earth's surface, correct to the nearest whole number.
Calculate the smallest possible area of land on the Earth's surface.
Give your answer in standard form to an appropriate degree of accuracy.

Q6 A train travels 65 kilometres (to the nearest kilometre) in a time of 35 minutes
(to the nearest minute). What are the maximum and minimum speeds of the train,
in kilometres per hour? Give your answer to an appropriate degree of accuracy.

The answers are given on pages 104–105.

Exam Questions and Answers

1 The table shows the mathematics test results for 90 pupils. The test was marked out of 60.

Mark (x)	Frequency	Cumulative frequency
$0 \leqslant x \leqslant 10$	12	12
$10 < x \leqslant 20$	15	27
$20 < x \leqslant 30$	29	56
$30 < x \leqslant 40$	16	72
$40 < x \leqslant 50$	11	83
$50 < x \leqslant 60$	7	90

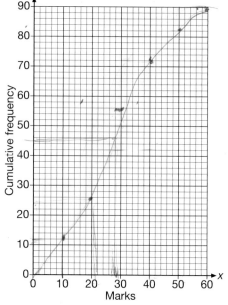

(a) Complete the cumulative frequency column.
(b) Draw a cumulative frequency diagram on the grid opposite.
(c) Use your diagram to estimate:
   (i) the median
   (ii) the inter-quartile range.
(d) The pass mark for the test is 25 marks. Use your graph to estimate how many pupils pass the test.

Answer

(a)

Mark (x)	Frequency	Cumulative frequency
$0 \leqslant x \leqslant 10$	12	12
$10 < x \leqslant 20$	15	27
$20 < x \leqslant 30$	29	56
$30 < x \leqslant 40$	16	72
$40 < x \leqslant 50$	11	83
$50 < x \leqslant 60$	7	90

(b) See the graph opposite.

(c) (i) median = 26

   (ii) IQR = 19

(d) 48

How to score full marks

● The cumulative frequency is a 'running total' of all the scores, so you need to add on the frequency each time.

● For the cumulative frequency diagram, plot the cumulative frequency against the upper value of the class.

● Read the values from the graph.

   (i) the median (at the 45th value) = 26

   (ii) the inter-quartile range (the difference between the upper quartile and the lower quartile) = 36 − 17 = 19

● From the graph, 42 pupils have fewer than 25 marks, so 90 − 42 = 48 pupils pass the test.

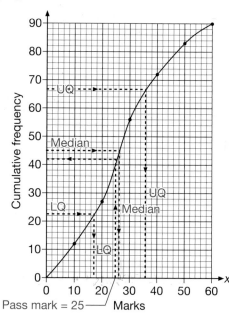

Key points to remember

The range

You can find the range of a distribution by working out the difference between the greatest value and least value.

Interquartile range

The interquartile range only takes account of the middle 50% of the distribution. You can find the interquartile range by dividing the data into four parts and working out the difference between the upper quartile and the lower quartile.

data listed in order

lower quartile   median   upper quartile

|←   interquartile range   →|

Finding the values

If there are n values in the distribution then:

- the median is the $\frac{1}{2}(n + 1)$th value
- the lower quartile is the $\frac{1}{4}(n + 1)$th value
- the upper quartile is the $\frac{3}{4}(n + 1)$th value

When n is large (say around 50) then:

- the median is the $\frac{1}{2}n$th value
- the lower quartile is the $\frac{1}{4}n$th value
- the upper quartile is the $\frac{3}{4}n$th value

Cumulative frequency diagrams

You can find the cumulative frequency by calculating the accumulated (or running) totals of the frequencies. Plot these against the upper class boundaries, then join up the points with a smooth curve to draw the cumulative frequency diagram (or ogive).

You must plot the points very carefully – the curve usually needs to be accurate to within $\pm \frac{1}{2}$ square.

Don't make these mistakes ...

Don't lose easy marks – always present the range as a single value (for example, 7 not 11–18).

Remember to plot the points at the upper class boundaries – which is the highest value that the interval can take.

Always check that the accumulated (or running) totals add up correctly.

All cumulative frequency curves have this shape.

Q1 These are the heights of 15 bushes.

13 cm, 36 cm, 16 cm, 13 cm, 21 cm, 37 cm, 38 cm, 18 cm, 37 cm, 19 cm, 12 cm, 20 cm, 18 cm, 20 cm, 10 cm

Find the range and interquartile range.

Q2 The table shows the lifetime of batteries given to the nearest hour.

Draw a cumulative frequency curve to illustrate this information and use your graph to find:

(a) how many batteries lasted less than 250 hours

(b) how many batteries lasted more than 350 hours

(c) the median and the interquartile range.

Lifetime (hours)	Frequency
100–199	32
200–299	98
300–399	65
400–499	14
500–599	3
600–699	2

Q3 The speed in miles per hour (mph) of 200 cars travelling on a road were measured.

The results are shown in the table.

(a) Draw a cumulative frequency curve to show these figures.

(b) Use your graph to find an estimate for:

(i) the median speed (in mph)

(ii) the interquartile range (in mph)

(iii) the percentage of cars travelling at less than 48 miles per hour.

Speed (mph)	Cumulative frequency
not exceeding 20	1
not exceeding 25	5
not exceeding 30	14
not exceeding 35	28
not exceeding 40	66
not exceeding 45	113
not exceeding 50	164
not exceeding 55	196
not exceeding 60	200
Total	200

Q4 Michelle has to escort a coach party of 48 people.

She arrives at the coach station at 7 a.m.

She keeps a record of the time, t minutes, she has been waiting before people arrive.

Time (t) minutes	$5 \leq t < 10$	$10 \leq t < 15$	$15 \leq t < 20$	$20 \leq t < 25$
Frequency	0	2	4	7
Time (t) minutes	$25 \leq t < 30$	$30 \leq t < 35$	$35 \leq t < 40$	$40 \leq t < 45$
Frequency	15	14	5	1

(a) Complete the cumulative frequency table.

Time	$t < 10$							
Frequency	0							

(b) On the graph paper provided, draw a cumulative frequency diagram for the data.

(c) Find the median arrival time.

(d) Petra is the twelfth person to arrive.
  (i) Estimate her time of arrival.
  (ii) The coach arrived when three-quarters of the passengers were there.
      How long did Petra wait before the coach arrived?

(e) Karen arrived at 7:32 a.m.
    How many people arrived after Karen?

Cumulative frequency
Length of time (minutes)

Q5 In a school survey, the heights of 80 boys aged 14 years are recorded.

The cumulative frequency graph shows the results.

(a) What is the median height of the boys?

(b) What is the interquartile range of the boys' heights?

The heights of 80 girls aged 14 are also recorded.

For the girls' heights:

    the median is 162 cm

    the lower quartile is 156 cm

    the upper quartile is 168 cm

    the shortest girl is 143 cm

    the tallest girl is 182 cm.

Cumulative frequency
Boys
Height (cm)

(c) (i) Use this information to draw, on the same diagram, a suitable cumulative frequency graph for the heights of the girls.

    (ii) Compare and comment on the heights of these boys and girls.

The answers are given on pages 105–107.

13 Mode, median and mean

Exam Questions and Answers

1 A student's test results are recorded as follows.

9   8   6   9   7   5   10   9   5   10

(a) Calculate:
   (i)   the mean mark
   (ii) the median mark
   (iii) the modal mark.

The student realises that one of the marks recorded as 5 should have been 6.

(b) What effect will this have on:
   (i)   the mean mark
   (ii) the median mark
   (iii) the modal mark?

Answer

(a) (i) Mean = 7.8

   (ii) Median = $\dfrac{8+9}{2}$ = 8.5

   (iii) Mode = 9

(b) (i) The mean mark will increase as the total mark increases slightly.

   (ii) The median mark stays the same as the order is not affected, so the middle numbers are the same.

   (iii) The modal mark stays the same as 9 is still the number that occurs most frequently.

How to score full marks

- The mean = $\dfrac{78}{10}$ = 7.8

- Arrange the numbers in order to find the median:

   5 5 6 7 8 9 9 9 10 10

   The median is the middle value = $\dfrac{8+9}{2}$ = 8.5

   The median is the $5\frac{1}{2}$th value, between the 5th and 6th.

- The mode is the value that appears most often and is 9.

- You need to explain briefly the effects you are describing but you do not need to recalculate.

2 The following table shows the numbers of words in 100 sentences of a particular book.

Number of words	Frequency f
1–5	15
6–10	29
11–15	25
16–20	15
21–25	11
26–30	2
31–35	1
36–40	0
41–45	2

(a) Write down:
  (i) the modal class interval
  (ii) the class interval in which the median lies.

(b) Work out an estimate of the mean number of words in a sentence.

Answer

(a) (i) Modal class interval
     = 6–10

   (ii) Median falls in the
        11–15 class.

(b) Estimated mean = 13

How to score full marks

- The modal class interval is the class with the greatest frequency. This is 6–10.
- The median is the $\frac{1}{2}(n+1)$th value $= \frac{1}{2} \times 101 = 50\frac{1}{2}$

  This falls in the 11–15 class.

Words	Frequency f	Mid-interval x	fx
1–5	15	3	45
6–10	29	8	232
11–15	25	13	325
16–20	15	18	270
21–25	11	23	253
26–30	2	28	56
31–35	1	33	33
36–40	0	38	0
41–45	2	43	86
	$\Sigma f = 100$		$\Sigma fx = 1300$

- Mean $= \frac{1300}{100} = 13$

Key points to remember

Mode
- The mode is the value that occurs most frequently.
- If there are two modes then the distribution is bimodal.
- If there are more than two modes then the distribution is multi-modal.

Bimodal distribution

Multimodal distribution

Mode of a frequency distribution
- The mode of frequency distribution is the value that has the highest frequency.
- The mode of a grouped frequency distribution is the group that has the highest frequency; this is called the modal group.

Mean
To find the mean of a distribution, find the total of the values of the distribution and divide by the number of values. The definition is often written as:

$$\text{mean} = \frac{\text{total of the values}}{\text{number of values}}$$

Median of a frequency distribution
You can usually find the median of a frequency distribution or a group frequency distribution from a cumulative frequency distribution. See *Chapter 12, Cumulative frequency* for more information.

Median
- The median is the middle value when the values are arranged in order.
- Where there are two middle values, you add the two numbers and divide by 2.
- If there are n values in the distribution then the median position is given by the $\frac{1}{2}(n + 1)$th value.

Mean of a frequency distribution
To find the mean of a frequency distribution, find the total of the values of the distribution (Σfx) and divide by the number of values (Σf).

$$\text{mean} = \frac{\Sigma fx}{\Sigma f}$$

Mean of a grouped frequency distribution
To find the mean of a grouped frequency distribution, use the mid-interval values or midpoints.

To find the mean of a grouped frequency distribution, find the total of the values of the frequency × mid-interval values of the distribution, then divide by the number of values.

$$\text{mean} = \frac{\text{total of (frequency} \times \text{mid-interval values)}}{\text{number of values}} = \frac{\Sigma fx}{\Sigma f}$$

Don't make these mistakes ...

You could lose marks by giving silly answers. Make sure your answers are realistic.

Don't guess at the mid-interval value. It is found by taking the mean of the upper and lower class boundaries.

Don't forget that the mid-interval values are used as an estimate of the particular interval, so the final answer will not be exact but will be an 'estimate of the mean'.

Q1 A set of 25 times, in seconds, is recorded.

12.9	10.0	4.2	16.0	5.6	18.1	8.3	14.0	11.5	21.7
22.2	6.0	13.6	3.1	11.5	10.8	15.7	3.7	9.4	8.0
6.4	17.0	7.3	12.8	13.5					

(a) Complete the frequency table below, using intervals of 5 seconds.

Time (t) seconds	Tally	Frequency
$0 \leqslant t < 5$		

(b) Write down the modal class interval.

Q2 David is playing cricket.

The table shows the number of runs he has scored off each ball so far.

Number of runs	0	1	2	3	4	5	6
Number of balls	3	8	4	3	5	0	2

(a) (i) What is the median number of runs per ball?

(ii) Calculate the mean number of runs per ball.

Off the next five balls, David scores the following numbers of runs.

4, 4, 5, 3 and 6

(b) (i) Calculate the new median.

(ii) Calculate the new mean.

(c) Give a reason why the mean is used, rather than the median, to give the average number of runs scored per ball.

Q3 (a) Pauline measures the lengths of some English cucumbers.

These are the lengths, in centimetres.

27, 28, 29, 30, 31, 31, 32, 33, 35, 37, 39

(i) What is the range of the lengths of these cucumbers?

(ii) What is the mean length of these cucumbers?

Pauline measures the lengths of some Spanish cucumbers. The range of the lengths of these cucumbers is 6 cm and the mean is 30 cm.

(b) Comment on the differences in these two varieties of cucumber.

Q4 The label on a jar of honey states that it contains 454 grams of honey.

The actual weight of honey in each of 20 jars was checked.

The results are shown in the table.

(a) Work out the range of the weights in the table.

(b) Calculate the mean weight of honey per jar.

Weight (g)	Number of jars
454	0
455	1
456	6
457	7
458	3
459	1
460	2

Q5 On holiday Val records the length of time people stay in a pool.

The results are shown in the table.

Calculate an estimate of the mean time spent in the pool.

Give your answer to an appropriate degree of accuracy.

Time, t (mins)	Number of people
$0 < t \leqslant 10$	4
$10 < t \leqslant 20$	7
$20 < t \leqslant 30$	3
$30 < t \leqslant 40$	2
Total	16

Q6 The following table shows the heights of plants.

Calculate an estimate of the mean height.

Height (cm)	15–20	20–30	30–40	40–50	50–60	60–70	70–80
Frequency	8	4	5	11	17	2	1

Q7 A manufacturer of school coats produces sizes according to height.

He measures the heights of 60 boys, with the following results.

Height, h (cm)	Frequency
$140 \leqslant h < 148$	6
$148 \leqslant h < 156$	10
$156 \leqslant h < 164$	15
$164 \leqslant h < 172$	18
$172 \leqslant h < 180$	11

(a) Calculate an estimate of the mean height of the boys.

(b) Explain how you can tell that the median lies between 156 cm and 164 cm.

(c) On a grid as shown, draw a histogram to display the data.

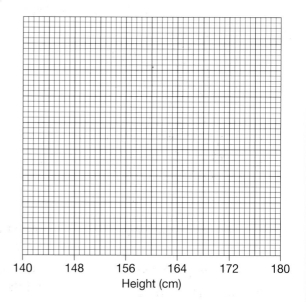

140   148   156   164   172   180

Height (cm)

The answers are given on pages 107–110.

14 Scatter diagrams

1 Nicky compared the scores awarded by two judges in a gymnastics competition. Here are their scores for 10 competitors.

Judge 1	2.3	7.3	7.7	4.4	8.5	7.7	1.8	8.1	1.9	7.0
Judge 2	2.4	7.5	6.9	4.7	8.7	7.9	2.3	7.8	5.1	6.5

(a) Complete the scatter graph for these data. The first four points have been plotted for you.

(b) Describe fully the correlation between the two sets of scores.

(c) (i) Draw the line of best fit on the graph.

(ii) Estimate the score from Judge 2 for a competitor given 5.6 by Judge 1.

Answer

(a)

(b) The correlation is strongly positive.

(c) (i) See the graph above.

(ii) Judge 2's score would be 5.7.

How to score full marks

- Use the data to complete the scatter graph.

- Remember that you are asked to describe the correlation between the two sets of scores fully.

- Draw the line of best fit so that it passes through as many points as possible, with equal numbers of points on either side.

- Estimate the score from Judge 2 for a competitor given 5.6 by Judge 1.

Key points to remember

Scatter diagrams

Scatter diagrams (or scatter graphs) are graphs that are used to show the relationship between two variables. Each of the two variables is assigned to a different axis and the information is plotted as sets of coordinates.

Correlation

Scatter diagrams can be used to show whether there is any relationship or correlation between the two variables.

Little or no correlation

The points are scattered randomly over the graph, showing little or no correlation between the two variables.

Moderate correlation

The points lie close to a straight line, suggesting some correlation between the two variables (the closer the points are to forming a line, the stronger the correlation).

Strong correlation

The points lie almost along a straight line, showing a strong correlation between the two variables.

Correlation may also be positive or negative.

Positive correlation

Where an increase in one variable is associated with an increase in the other variable, the correlation is positive or direct.

Negative correlation

Where an increase in one variable is associated with a decrease in the other variable, the correlation is negative or inverse.

Line of best fit

If the points on a scatter diagram show moderate or strong correlation, a line can be drawn to approximate the relationship.

This is called the line of best fit (or regression line).

This line can be used to predict other values from the given data.

Don't make these mistakes ...

Always draw the line of best fit so that there are roughly equal numbers of points on either side of the line.

In most cases a line of best fit can be drawn 'by eye'.

The line of best fit does not have to pass through the origin.

For more accurate work, the line of best fit should pass through $(\bar{x}, \bar{y})$ where $\bar{x}$ and $\bar{y}$ are the mean values of x and y respectively.

Q1 The following table shows the heights and shoe sizes of 10 pupils.

Shoe size	3	2	5	$6\frac{1}{2}$	4	3	6	1	$3\frac{1}{2}$	$7\frac{1}{2}$
Height (cm)	132	125	149	157	134	127	151	117	141	100

Plot this information on a graph and comment on your findings.

Q2 The table shows the relationship between pupils' arm lengths and the distances they can throw an object.

(a) Plot this information on a graph and draw the line of best fit.

(b) Use the line of best fit to estimate:
   (i) the distance thrown by someone with an arm length of 50 cm
   (ii) the arm length when the distance an object is thrown is 5.5 m.

Arm length (cm)	Distance thrown (m)
40	4.9
36	4.2
33	3.0
46	5.7
43	4.8
41	4.6
47	6.0
52	6.1
45	5.4
33	3.6

Q3 The scatter diagram shows the height of some plants, *d* days after germinating.

Number of days after germination (*d*)

(a) Draw the line of best fit.
(b) Use your line of best fit to estimate the height of a plant:
   (i) 10 days after germination
   (ii) 20 days after germination.
(c) Which of your two answers in (b) is likely to be more reliable?
   Give a reason for your answer.

Q4 The table shows the 1961 figures for adult literacy and life expectancy in eight countries.

Country	Adult literacy %	Life expectancy (years)
Chile	88	63
Ethiopia	10	38
India	29	49
Iran	49	51
Italy	90	71
Malaysia	58	58
Paraguay	75	61
Saudi Arabia	15	45

(a) On the graph paper, draw a scatter graph of these figures.

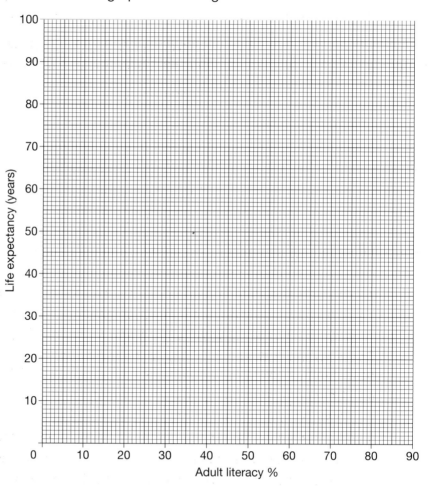

(b) From the scatter graph, state what correlation, if any, there is between 'Adult literacy' and the 'Life expectancy' figures.

(c) Draw a line of best fit.

Using this, estimate the life expectancy of an adult from a country with 42% adult literacy.

(d) Do you think that it is a good idea to draw conclusions from this set of figures? Give a reason for your answer.

The answers are given on pages 110–112.

Exam Questions and Answers

1   Six events are given below.

Select a letter on the probability scale on the right which best shows the probability of these events happening.

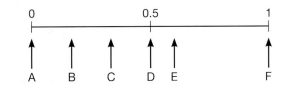

(i)   throwing a six on a fair die
(ii) a newborn baby being a boy
(iii) selecting a month with 31 days from the calendar
(iv) February will have 31 days next year
(v)   there will be 30 days in June
(vi) selecting a chocolate from a bag containing one mint, one chocolate and one jelly sweet

Answer

(i)   B

(ii) D

(iii) E

(iv) A

(v)   F

(vi) C

How to score full marks

- p(throwing a six) = $\frac{1}{6}$
- p(a newborn baby being a boy) = $\frac{1}{2}$
- p(selecting a month with 31 days from the calendar) = $\frac{7}{12}$
- p(February will have 31 days next year) = 0
- p(30 days in June) = 1
- p(selecting a chocolate) = $\frac{1}{3}$

2   A box contains buttons.

The buttons have two, three or four holes as shown.
The buttons are coloured white or red or green.
A button is taken at random from the box.
The table shows the probabilities of the number of holes and the colours of the buttons.

		Number of holes		
		2	3	4
	White	0.3	0.2	0
Colour	Red	0.1	0	0.2
	Green	0	0.1	0.1

(a) A button is taken from the box at random.

What is the probability that:

(i)   it is red with two holes   (ii) it has two holes

(iii) it is red or has two holes (or both)   (iv) it has four holes?

(b) The box contains 50 buttons. How many buttons have four holes?

Answer

(a) (i)   0.1
     (ii) 0.4
     (iii) 0.6
     (iv) 0.3

(b) 15

How to score full marks

- p(red with two holes) = 0.1 (from table)
- p(two holes) = 0.3 + 0.1 + 0 = 0.4
- p(red or two holes) = 0.1 + 0 + 0.2 + 0.3 + 0 (don't count 0.1 twice)
- p(four holes) = 0 + 0.2 + 0.1 = 0.3
- The number with four holes will be 50 × 0.3 = 15.

Key points to remember

Probability

impossible   evens   certainty

$$0 \qquad \tfrac{1}{2} \qquad 1$$

In probability:

- an event that is certain to happen has a probability of 1
- an event that is impossible has a probability of 0.

In general, $p(\text{success}) = \dfrac{\text{number of 'successful' outcomes}}{\text{number of 'possible' outcomes}}$

where p(success) means the probability of success.

Total probability

p(an event happening)
= 1 − p(an event not happening)

p(an event not happening)
= 1 − p(an event happening)

so p(an event happening)
+ p(an event not happening) = 1

Tree diagrams

In a tree diagram, the probabilities of events are written on different branches.

The total sum of the probabilities at the ends of all the branches must equal 1.

Possibility spaces

A possibility space is a diagram which can be used to show the outcomes of various events.

Addition rule for mutually exclusive events

Events are mutually exclusive if they cannot happen at the same time. For example, a playing card cannot be both a spade and a red card.

For mutually exclusive events, you can apply the addition rule (also called the **or** rule):

p(A or B) = p(A) + p(B)

Remember that to add fractions you must have a common denominator.

Multiplication rule – independent events

Events are independent if one event does not affect the other event. For example, if you toss a coin and pick a card, neither event affects the result of the other.

For independent events, you can use the multiplication rule (also called the **and** rule):

p(A and B) = p(A) × p(B)

Remember that to multiply fractions you multiply the numerators and you multiply the denominators.

Don't make these mistakes ...

Probabilities greater than 1 or less than 0 do not have any meaning.

Probabilities can be expressed as fractions, decimals or percentages but not as ratios.

Q1 (a) A bag contains only red marbles and blue marbles.

Hugh chooses a marble without looking.

Under each of the statements, tick the appropriate box.

(i) The probability that the marble is red is $\frac{1}{2}$.

Must be correct ☐   Might be correct ☐   Must be wrong ☐

(ii) The probability that the marble is red or blue is 1.

Must be correct ☐   Might be correct ☐   Must be wrong ☐

(iii) The probability that the marble is red is −0.4.

Must be correct ☐   Might be correct ☐   Must be wrong ☐

(b) Another bag contains three red, four blue and five green marbles.

Hugh chooses a marble from this bag without looking.

What is the probability that it is:

(i) blue   (ii) blue or red   (iii) yellow?

Q2 The table shows the colour and make of 20 cars.

		Colour of car	
		White	**Blue**
Make of car	**Vauxhall**	7	4
	Ford	3	6

(a) A car is chosen at random.

What is the probability that it is a blue Ford?

(b) A white car is chosen at random.

What is the probability that it is a Vauxhall?

Q3 A record was kept of the number of occupants in cars arriving at a car park.

The numbers collected for 50 cars are shown in the bar chart.

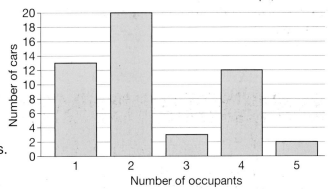

(a) One of these cars is chosen at random. Find the probability that it arrived with two occupants.

(b) Find the total number of car occupants.

(c) One of the car occupants is chosen at random.

Find the probability that the person:

(i) was driving a car as it arrived at the car park

(ii) was a passenger from a car with four occupants.

Questions to try

Q4 (a) A fair coin is thrown 20 times. It lands heads 12 times.

What is the relative frequency of throwing a head?

The coin continues to be thrown. The table shows the number of heads recorded for 20, 40, 60, 80 and 100 throws.

Number of throws	20	40	60	80	100
Number of heads	12	18	30	42	49

(b) Draw a graph to show the relative frequency of throwing a head for these data.

(c) Estimate the relative frequency of throwing a head for 1000 throws.

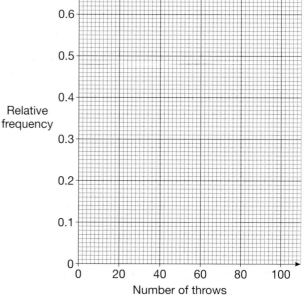

Q5 The diagram shows two spinners.

Spinner A has four equal sectors and spinner B has six equal sectors.

The sectors are numbered as shown.

Each spinner is spun once, spinner A followed by spinner B.

(a) Complete the tree diagram for both spinners.

(b) What is the probability of getting a score of 3 with each spinner?

(c) The scores on the two spinners are added.

What is the probability of getting a total score of 5?

Spinner A   **Spinner B**

Spinner A   **Spinner B**

Q6   In a game, Paula spins two fair five-sided spinners at the same time.
Her total score is the sum of the scores on the two spinners.

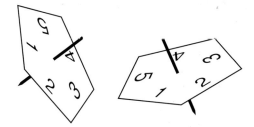

(a)   What is the probability that Paula scores a total of 10 on her next spin?
(b)   What is the probability that she scores a total of 9 on her next spin?
(c)   What is the probability that the total score on her next spin is 3 or less?
(d)   In another game, three of these spinners are used. What is the probability that all three of them show a five on the next spin?

Q7   Here is a five-sided spinner.
Its sides are labelled 1, 2, 3, 4, 5.
Alan spins the spinner and throws a coin.
One possible outcome is (3, Heads).
(a)   List all the possible outcomes.

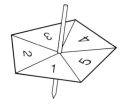

The spinner is biased.
The probability that the spinner will land on each of the numbers 1 to 4 is given in the table.

Number	1	2	3	4	5
Probability	0.36	0.1	0.25	0.15	

Alan spins the spinner once.
(b)   (i)   Work out the probability that the spinner will land on 5.
       (ii) Write down the probability that the spinner will land on 6.
       (iii) Write down the number that the spinner is most likely to land on.
       (iv) Work out the probability that the spinner will land on an even number.
Alan spins the spinner and throws a fair coin.
(c)   Work out the probability that the spinner will land on 3 and the coin will show Heads.

The answers are given on pages 112–114.

Exam Questions and Answers

1 A farmer weighs all 60 eggs collected on Monday. The results are summarised in the grouped frequency distribution below.

Mass, x grams	Number of eggs, f	Frequency density
$30 \leqslant x < 50$	5	
$50 \leqslant x < 60$	15	
$60 \leqslant x < 90$	30	
$90 \leqslant x < 110$	10	

(a) Complete the frequency density column in the table and draw a histogram of the data in the table.

(b) The next day, Tuesday, the farmer again weighs all the eggs collected. The results are shown in the histogram on the left.

(i) Use this histogram to calculate how many eggs were collected on Tuesday.

(ii) Estimate the mass that is exceeded by 50% of the eggs on Tuesday.

Answer

(a)

Mass, x grams	Number of eggs, f	Frequency density
$30 \leq x < 50$	5	0.25
$50 \leq x < 60$	15	1.5
$60 \leq x < 90$	30	1
$90 \leq x < 110$	10	0.5

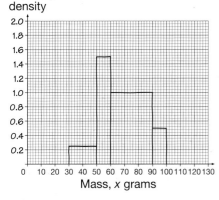

(b) (i) 40

(ii) 75 g

How to score full marks

● Complete the frequency density column in the table, by calculating (frequency ÷ class width) for each row.

Mass, x grams	Number of eggs f	Class width	Frequency density
$30 \leq x < 50$	5	20	$5 \div 20 = 0.25$
$50 \leq x < 60$	15	10	$15 \div 10 = 1.5$
$60 \leq x < 90$	30	30	$30 \div 30 = 1$
$90 \leq x < 100$	10	20	$10 \div 20 = 0.5$

● Use the table to draw the histogram.

● (i) The number of eggs is the area of the bars in the histogram:
= $10 \times 0.4 + 20 \times 0.5 + 40 \times 0.4 + 10 \times 1 = 40$ eggs

(ii) To estimate the mass that is exceeded by 50% of the eggs on Tuesday, you need to draw a line to represent 20 eggs.

The line needs to be drawn $\frac{6}{16}$ along the interval.

The value is $60 + \frac{6}{16} \times 40 = 60 + 15 = 75$ g

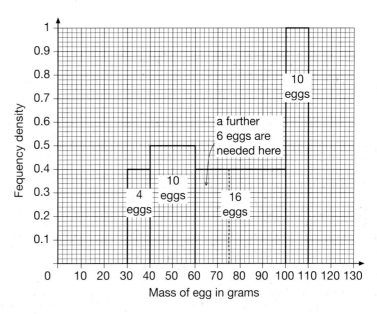

Key points to remember

Histograms

In histograms, the area of each bar represents the frequency so:

- **class width** × **height = frequency**

- **height =** $\dfrac{\text{frequency}}{\text{class width}}$

The height is the frequency density, so remember that the vertical axis of a histogram should be labelled frequency density and:

- **frequency density =** $\dfrac{\text{frequency}}{\text{class width}}$

For equal class intervals, the histogram looks like a bar chart.

Histograms and bar charts

They are alike if the bars are of equal width, but it is the **area** of each bar that represents the frequency.

Frequency polygons

A frequency polygon can be drawn from a histogram by joining the midpoints of the tops of the bars with straight lines to form a polygon.

The lines should be extended to the horizontal axis on either side so that the area under the frequency polygon is the same as the area under the histogram.

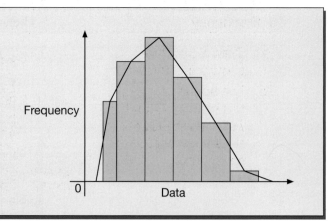

Don't make these mistakes ...

Histograms look like bar charts but don't forget that it is the area of each 'bar' that represents the frequency, not the length or height.

The bars on the horizontal axis should be drawn at the class boundaries for measured quantities such as heights and masses.

Q1 One hundred teenagers were asked how much television they had watched the previous evening.

The results of the survey are shown in the table below.

Time t (hours)	Frequency
$0 \leqslant t < 0.5$	16
$0.5 \leqslant t < 1$	28
$1 \leqslant t < 2$	26
$2 \leqslant t < 3$	12
$3 \leqslant t < 5$	18

Draw a histogram to illustrate the results.

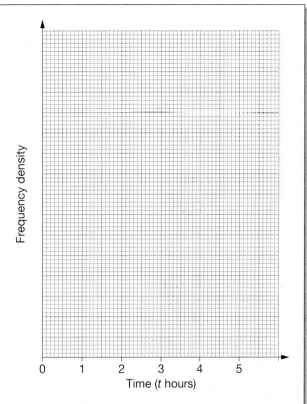

Q2 The speeds of 100 cars travelling along a road are shown in the table.

Speed (s km/h)	$20 \leqslant s < 35$	$35 \leqslant s < 45$	$45 \leqslant s < 55$	$55 \leqslant s < 65$	$65 \leqslant s < 85$
Frequency	6	19	34	26	15

(a) Draw a histogram to show this information.

(b) The speed limit along this road is 48 km/h. Estimate the number of cars exceeding the speed limit.

Q3 The frequency distribution shows the heights of 50 plants measured to the nearest centimetre.

Draw a frequency polygon to represent this information.

Height (cm)	Frequency
15–19	4
20–24	6
25–29	7
30–39	11
40–49	9
50–74	5
75–99	2

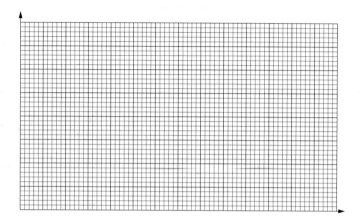

Q4 The table gives the prices (in pounds) of all 53 models of digital cameras available in British shops in December 1997.

(a) Estimate the mean price of the cameras.

(b) Draw a histogram to illustrate the prices in December 1997.

Price (£p)	Frequency
$0 \leqslant p < 200$	6
$200 \leqslant p < 400$	21
$400 \leqslant p < 600$	17
$600 \leqslant p < 1000$	7
$1000 \leqslant p < 2000$	2

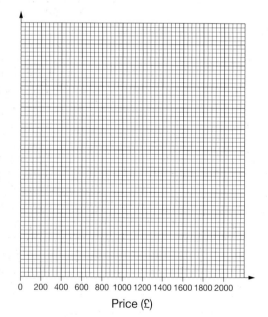

Price (£)

The histogram below shows the prices of all digital cameras in British shops in May 1997.

(c) How many cameras were available in May 1997?

(d) Compare, in two ways, the prices of cameras in December 1997 with the prices in May 1997.

Price (£)

Q5 A company manufactures various types of lightbulbs. One type of bulb manufactured by the company is considered to be environmentally friendly since bulbs of this type have a long lifetime.

Lifetime, x (1000s hours)	Number of bulbs, f	Frequency density
$6 \leq x < 10$	4	
$10 \leq x < 12$	15	
$12 \leq x < 14$	19	
$14 \leq x < 16$	8	
$16 \leq x < 20$	4	

The lifetimes, in thousands of hours, of a sample of 50 bulbs of this type are measured and the results are summarised in the grouped frequency distribution on the right.

(a) Complete the frequency density column in the table and draw a histogram of the data in the table.

(b) Another company also manufactures an environmentally-friendly light bulb. The lifetimes, in thousands of hours, of a sample of these bulbs are also measured. The results are shown in the histogram on the right.

Estimate the proportion of the light bulbs manufactured by the second company that last longer than 15 000 hours.

(c) By comparing the two histograms, and giving a reason for your answer, comment on which of the two companies manufactures the most environmentally-friendly light bulbs.

The answers are given on pages 114–117.

Exam Questions and Answers

1 A bag contains five red and four blue counters. A counter is drawn from the bag and then a second counter is drawn from the bag. Draw a tree diagram to show the various possibilities that can occur and use the diagram to find the probability that both counters are blue.

Answer

With replacement:

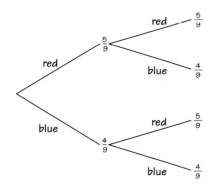

$p(\text{blue, blue}) = \frac{16}{81}$

Without replacement:

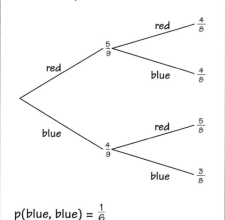

$p(\text{blue, blue}) = \frac{1}{6}$

How to score full marks

The question does not make it clear whether the first counter is replaced before the second counter is drawn. This gives rise to two possibilities.

With replacement (independent events)

● Where the first counter is replaced before the second counter is drawn then the two events are independent and the probabilities for each event are the same.

● You should have a diagram as shown on the left.

● From the diagram, the probability that both counters are blue, p(blue, blue), is p(blue counter drawn first and blue counter drawn second)

= p(blue counter drawn first) × p(blue counter drawn second)

$= \frac{4}{9} \times \frac{4}{9}$

$= \frac{16}{81}$

Without replacement (dependent events)

● Where the first counter is not replaced before the second counter is drawn then the two events are not independent (i.e. they are dependent) and the probabilities for the second event will be affected by the outcomes of the first event.

● For the second counter then:

if the first counter was red, there are still 4 blue counters and 8 counters altogether

if the first counter was blue, there are now 3 blue counters and 8 counters altogether.

● You should have a diagram as shown on the left.

● From the diagram you can see that the probability that both counters are blue, p(blue, blue)

= p(blue counter drawn first and blue counter drawn second)

= p(blue counter drawn first) × p(blue counter drawn second)

$= \frac{4}{9} \times \frac{3}{8}$

$= \frac{12}{72}$

$= \frac{1}{6}$

Probability

In probability, an event that is certain to happen has a probability of 1 whereas an event that is impossible has a probability of 0.

In general:

$$p(\text{success}) = \frac{\text{number of 'successful' outcomes}}{\text{number of possible outcomes}}$$

where p(success) means the probability of success.

Addition rule – mutually exclusive events

Events are mutually exclusive if they cannot happen at the same time.

For mutually exclusive events, use the addition rule (also called the **or** rule):

P(A or B) = p(A) + p(B)

Remember that to add fractions you must first find a common denominator.

Multiplication rule – independent events

Events are **independent** if one event does not affect the other.

For independent events, use the multiplication rule (also called the **and** rule):

p(A and B) = p(A) × p(B)

Remember that to multiply fractions you multiply the numerators and you multiply the denominators.

Don't make these mistakes ...

Don't discount zeros in decimal fractions!

0.1 × 0.1 = 0.01

0.2 × 0.2 = 0.04

0.3 × 0.3 = 0.09 ...

Don't forget

Probabilities greater than 1 or less than 0 do not have any meaning.

Q1 A bag contains four red and six blue balls. One ball is chosen at random and its colour is noted. The ball is not replaced and a second ball is chosen at random and its colour is noted. Draw a tree diagram to represent this situation and use it to calculate:

(a) the probability of obtaining two red balls

(b) the probability of obtaining one ball of each colour.

Q2 A box contains five red discs, four blue discs, two white discs and one black disc. Three discs are drawn at random without replacement from the box.
Calculate the probability that:

(a) the three discs drawn are red

(b) the three discs drawn are of the same colour

(c) exactly two of the discs drawn are red.

Q3 Q, R and S are three mutually exclusive events where p(event Q) = 30%, p(event R) = $\frac{1}{4}$ and p(event S) = 0.2.
Calculate the probability of:

(a) either Q or R occurring

(b) either R or S occurring

(c) any of Q or R or S occurring.

Q4 A biased six-sided die is such that a score of 6 is twice as likely as a score of 5. A score of 5 is twice as likely as a score of 4. The probabilities of a score of 1, 2, 3 and 4 are all the same.
Calculate the probability of:

(a) a score of 6

(b) a score of 5

(c) a score less than 4.

Q5 Miss Mutch travels to work by train or by coach. When she is travelling by train there is a 70% chance that she will complete the crossword in her newspaper but when she is travelling by coach there is a smaller chance that she will complete the crossword. On a work-day chosen at random the probability that she travels by train is 80%.

(a) Construct a tree diagram to illustrate (as far as is possible) the combined probability of the events 'travelling by train/coach' and 'completing her crossword'.

(b) Calculate the probability that on a work-day chosen at random Miss Mutch travels by train but does not complete her crossword.

(c) On a work-day chosen at random there is a 65% chance that Miss Mutch completes her crossword. Calculate the chance of Miss Mutch completing her crossword on a day when she travels by coach.

The answers are given on pages 117–119.

18 Patterns and sequences

Exam Questions and Answers

1   (a) Write down:
   (i)   the 8th term and
   (ii) the nth term of this sequence.
      1   5   9   13   17   …
   (b) Use your answer to (a) to write down the nth term of this sequence.
      1   25   81   169   289   …

Answer

(a) (i)   29

   (ii) nth term = $4n - 3$

(b) nth term = $(4n - 3)^2$

How to score full marks

- You should be able to find the 8th term quite easily, by counting on in the pattern (add 4 each time).

   1   5   9   13   17   21   25   29

- The sequence is formed by adding on the same number each time, so the first differences are all the same. This means the sequence is linear. As each term is found by 'adding on 4', the nth term must have something to do with $4n$. The first term is 1, so the rule is $4n - 3$.

- The question asks you to use the first sequence. If you look carefully, you will see that each term of the second sequence is the square of the equivalent term in the first sequence.

- The nth term is therefore the square of the nth term in the first sequence.

2   (a) A sequence of patterns is shown.

Pattern 1   Pattern 2   Pattern 3

Write an expression, in terms of n, for the number of white squares in the nth pattern of the sequence.

(b) A number sequence begins:

    3,   6,   11,   18,   27, ...

Write an expression, in terms of n, for the nth term of this sequence.

Answer

(a) nth term $= n + n + 3$

           $= 2n + 3$

(b) nth term $= n^2 + 2$

How to score full marks

- You can use the geometrical properties of the patterns to find the solution.

  For example the 4th pattern (pattern 4) gives:

  and the 5th pattern (pattern 5) gives:

  so the nth pattern gives:

  i.e. $n + n + 3$ or $2n + 3$

- Look at the sequence.

Sequence	3		6		11		18		27		...
1st difference		+3		+5		+7		+9		...	
2nd difference			+2		+2		+2		...		

- As the first differences are not the same, you need to work out the second differences. These are the same so the sequence is quadratic.

n^2	1	4	9	16	25	
Sequence	3	6	11	18	27	...

- Each term of the sequence is equal to $n^2 + 2$ so this is the nth term.

Key points to remember

Definition: A **sequence** is a set of numbers that follow a particular rule.

Linear sequences

For the sequence 3, 7, 11, 15, 19, ... you can work out the differences as shown.

Sequence	3	7	11	15	19	...
First difference		+4	+4	+4	+4	...

The first differences are all the same, so the sequence is linear and you can use:

nth term = first term + $(n - 1)$ × first difference

$= 3 + (n - 1) \times 4$

$= 3 + 4n - 4$

$= 4n - 1$

Quadratic sequences

Quadratic sequences will be limited to variations on n^2.

Sequence	**nth term**
1, 4, 9, 16, ...	n^2
2, 5, 10, 17, ...	$n^2 + 1$
0, 3, 8, 15, ...	$n^2 - 1$
2, 8, 18, 32, ...	$2n^2$

Don't make these mistakes ...

Don't forget that the nth term must work for all of the given values, not just the first one or two.

Don't jump in and use the formulae for linear and quadratic equations before you have tried to find an obvious simple answer to the sequence.

Don't miss patterns where some numbers seem to be missing from the sequence, e.g. 4, 9, 16, 25, ...
This is based on the square numbers but the nth term is not n^2 but $(n + 1)^2$.

Don't write out individual values for sequences in diagram form – they can usually be solved by looking at the geometrical shapes in the diagram.

Q1 Write down the first five terms of a sequence where the *nth* term is given as:

(a) $2n - 1$ (b) $n^2 - n$ (c) $\dfrac{n}{n+1}$

Q2 (a) What is the next number in this sequence?

3, 7, 11, 15, … .

One number in the sequence is x.

(b) (i) Write, in terms of x, the next number in the sequence.

(ii) Write, in terms of x, the number in the sequence before x.

Q3 Write down the *nth* term for each of the following sequences.

(a) 3, 6, 9, 12, …

(b) 1, 4, 7, 10, …

(c) 1, 4, 9, 16, …

(d) 4, 16, 36, 64, …

Q4 (a) Write down the next two terms of the following sequence.

2, 5, 11, 23, 47, …

(b) Explain how you get from one term of the sequence to the next term.

(c) Write down an expression for the *nth* term of this sequence.

$\dfrac{1}{4}, \dfrac{2}{5}, \dfrac{3}{6}, \dfrac{4}{7}, \dfrac{5}{8}, \dots$

Q5 (a) A sequence begins 2, 5, 8, 11, … .

Write an expression for the *nth* term of the sequence.

(b) The *nth* term of a different sequence is $\frac{1}{2}(n^2 - 2n)$.

(i) Write down the first term and the second term of the sequence.

(ii) When the *nth* term of the sequence is 40, the value of n can be found by solving the equation $n^2 - 2n - 80 = 0$.

Solve this equation and hence find the value of n.

You must show all your working.

Q6 Study the patterns of black and white squares shown below.

(a) How many white squares are there in the 4th pattern?

(b) Write an expression, in terms of n, for the number of white squares in the *nth* pattern.

  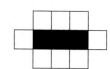

Q7 A sequence of matchstick patterns is shown below.

Write an expression, in terms of n, for the number of matchsticks in the *nth* pattern of the sequence.

The answers are given on pages 119–120.

19 Manipulation of equations

Exam Questions and Answers

1 Make l the subject of the formula $T = 2\pi\sqrt{\dfrac{l}{g}}$.

Answer

$$T = 2\pi\sqrt{\frac{l}{g}}$$

$$\frac{T}{2\pi} = \sqrt{\frac{l}{g}}$$

$$\left(\frac{T}{2\pi}\right)^2 = \frac{l}{g}$$

$$g\left(\frac{T}{2\pi}\right)^2 = l$$

$$l = g\left(\frac{T}{2\pi}\right)^2$$

How to score full marks

- Divide both sides of the formula by 2π.
- Square both sides (to get rid of the $\sqrt{}$ sign).
- Multiply both sides of the formula by g to isolate l.
- Turn the formula around so that l is the subject.

2 Solve the following equation.
$$\frac{2x - 3}{6} + \frac{x + 2}{3} = \frac{5}{2}$$

Answer

$$\frac{2x - 3}{6} + \frac{x + 2}{3} = \frac{5}{2}$$

$$\frac{2x - 3}{6} + \frac{2x + 2}{6} = \frac{15}{6}$$

$$2x - 3 + 2(x + 2) = 15$$

$$2x - 3 + 2x + 4 = 15$$

$$4x + 1 = 15$$

$$4x = 14$$

$$x = 3.5 \text{ or } 3\tfrac{1}{2}$$

How to score full marks

- To solve questions involving algebraic fractions, you need to change all the terms to fractions with the same (common) denominator.

- $\dfrac{2x-3}{6} + \dfrac{x+2}{3} = \dfrac{5}{2}$ $\dfrac{x+2}{3} = \dfrac{2(x+2)}{6}$ $\dfrac{5}{2} = \dfrac{15}{6}$

$\dfrac{2x-3}{6} + \dfrac{2(x+2)}{6} = \dfrac{15}{6}$ (writing all the terms with a denominator of 6)

$2x - 3 + 2(x + 2) = 15$ (multiplying throughout by 6)

$2x - 3 + 2x + 4 = 15$ (simplifying)

$4x + 1 = 15$ (simplifying further)

$4x = 14$

$x = \dfrac{14}{4} = 3.5 \text{ or } 3\tfrac{1}{2}$ (solving to find the value of x)

Key points to remember

Doing and undoing

Every mathematical operation has an inverse. You can use the inverse to 'undo' an equation or formula.

Operation	Inverse
add 5	subtract 5
subtract 3	add 3
multiply by 7	divide by 7 (or multiply by $\frac{1}{7}$)
divide by 4	multiply by 4
square	take the square root
take the square root	square

$a + 5 = 7$
$a + 5 - 5 = 7 - 5$ (as $+5 - 5 = 0$ and $a + 0 = a$)
$a = 2$
$b - 3 = 9$
$b - 3 + 3 = 9 + 3$ (as $-3 + 3 + 0$ and $b + 0 = b$)
$b = 12$
$c \times 7 = 21$
$c \times 7 \div 7 = 21 \div 7$ (as $7 \div 7 = 1$ and $c \times 1 = c$)
$c = 3$
$d \div 4 = 11$
$d \div 4 \times 4 = 11 \times 4$ (as $\div 4 \times 4 = 1$ and $d \times 1 = d$)
$d = 44$
$e^2 = 49$
$\sqrt{e^2} = \sqrt{49}$
$e = 7$
$\sqrt{f} = 10$
$(\sqrt{f})^2 = 10^2$
$f = 100$

Rearranging formulae

You can rearrange (or transpose) a formula in exactly the same way as you solve an equation. You must always keep the formula balanced, so you must make sure that whatever you do to one side, you also do to the other side.

For the formula $S = \frac{D}{T}$, S is the subject of the formula.

The formula can be rearranged to make D or T the subject.

$S = \dfrac{D}{T}$

$D = S \times T$ or $D = ST$ (multiplying both sides of the formula by T)

Or, from $D = ST$:

$\dfrac{D}{S} = T$ (dividing both sides of the formula by S)

$T = \dfrac{D}{S}$ (turning the formula around)

Algebraic fractions

If you remember how to work with numerical fractions, you will be able to use the same methods to work out algebraic fractions.

For example:

$\frac{1}{3} + \frac{1}{5} + \frac{1}{6}$

To add these fractions, first express them all as equivalent fractions with a common denominator.

Remember that to make an equivalent fraction you multiply or divide the numerator and the denominator by the same number.

So $\frac{1}{3} + \frac{1}{5} + \frac{1}{6} = \frac{10}{30} + \frac{6}{30} + \frac{5}{30} = \frac{21}{30}$

Don't make these mistakes ...

To add fractions you must always make sure they are over a common denominator.

You can always find a common denominator by multiplying all the denominators together, but this denominator will not always be the lowest common denominator.

$\frac{1}{3} = \frac{10}{30}$ $\frac{1}{5} = \frac{6}{30}$ $\frac{1}{6} = \frac{5}{30}$

Q1 Rearrange the formula $r = 4pq - s$ to make:

(a) s the subject

(b) q the subject.

Q2 Make c the subject of the following equation.

$$\frac{bc^2}{d} = 6$$

Q3 A small paving slab weighs x kilograms.

A large paving slab weighs $(2x + 3)$ kilograms.

(a) Write an expression, in terms of x, for the total weight of 16 small slabs and 4 large slabs.

Give your answer in its simplest form.

The total weight of the slabs is 132 kilograms.

(b) Write down an equation and find the value of x.

Q4 The diagram shows a rectangle with length $3x + 2$ and width $2x$.

All measurements are given in centimetres.

The perimeter of the rectangle is P centimetres.

The area of the rectangle is A square centimetres.

(a) Write down an expression in its simplest form, in terms of x, for:

    (i) P (ii) A.

$P = 44$.

(b) Work out the value of A.

Q5 The diagram shows the side view of a set of steps.

(i) Write down an expression, in its simplest form, for the area, A, of the side of the steps.

(ii) The area of the side of the steps is $3240\,\text{cm}^2$ and the breadth, b, of each step is 36 cm. Calculate the height, h, of each step.

Q6 Neil buys 30 shares in a company. Each share costs £x.

(a) How much does Neil spend?

(b) He sells 10 shares when the price of each share has risen by £1.

How much does he receive?

(c) He sells the other 20 shares when the price of each share is double what he paid for it. How much does he receive for these 20 shares?

(d) Neil makes £70 profit.

Form an equation in x and solve it to find the original cost of a share.

The answers are given on pages 120–121.

Exam Questions and Answers

1 Solve these simultaneous equations.

$$x + 2y = 7$$
$$3x - 2y = 5$$

Answer

$$x + 2y = 7$$
$$3x - 2y = 5$$
$$4x = 12$$
$$x = 3$$

$$x + 2y = 7$$
$$3 + 2y = 7$$
$$2y = 4$$
$$y = 2$$

How to score full marks

- Where the terms in x or the terms in y are numerically equal, you need to use the method of elimination (eliminate the term in x or y by adding or subtracting the two equations).
- In this example the terms in y are numerically equal (and the signs are opposite) so add the two equations.
- You need to divide both sides by 4 to find the value of x.
- Substitute the value of x (= 3) into the first equation.
- Subtract 3 from both sides.
- Divide both sides by 2 to find the value of y.

2 Solve these simultaneous equations.

$$x + 4y = 11$$
$$2x + y = 1$$

Answer

$$x + 4y = 11$$
$$2x + y = 1$$

$$x + 4y = 11$$
$$x = 11 - 4y$$

$$2x + y = 1$$
$$2(11 - 4y) + y = 1$$
$$22 - 8y + y = 1$$
$$22 - 7y = 1$$

$$22 = 1 + 7y$$
$$21 = 7y$$
$$y = 3$$

$$x + 4y = 11$$
$$x + 4 \times 3 = 11$$
$$x + 12 = 11$$
$$x = -1$$

How to score full marks

- Where neither the terms in x nor the terms in y are numerically equal, you need to use the method of substitution (by making x or y the subject of one of the equations).
- Use the first equation to make x the subject, by subtracting $4y$ from both sides.
- Replace the value of x in the second equation by $11 - 4y$.
- Expand the left-hand side of the equation, then simplify it by collecting like terms to find the value of y.
- Substitute the value of y (= 3) into the first equation.
- Simplify it and solve it to find the value of x.

Key points to remember

You can solve simultaneous equations by **elimination or substitution** – think about which method you are going to use, before you start.

- Where the terms in x or the terms in y are numerically equal, use elimination to remove the term in x or y by adding or subtracting the two equations.
- Where neither the terms in x nor the terms in y are numerically equal, use the method of substitution by making x or y the subject of one of the equations.

You need to know these methods as you will not always be able to use a calculator, and trial and error methods rarely receive full marks (especially if you only give one solution).

For the **elimination method**, you need to add the equations if the signs are opposite and subtract the equations if the signs are the same.

For the **substitution method**, choose the subject carefully (preferably where there is a single term in x or a single term in y) even if this means using the second equation.

If you get **silly answers**, such as very large numbers or difficult fractions, **go back and check your working**.

Check your answers by **substituting them back into both equations** to make sure that you have not made any silly mistakes.

Don't make these mistakes ...

Don't panic if the examination paper uses different letters.

$$a + 2b = 7$$
$$3a - 2b = 5$$

Use the method described above but remember the answers will be $a = \ldots$ and $b = \ldots$

When using the elimination method, watch out for negative signs.

$$4x - y = 7$$
$$4x - 2y = 4$$

gives:

$$-y - (-2y) = 7 - 4$$

Use brackets to help you.

$$-y + 2y = 3$$
$$y = 3$$

Q1 Solve these simultaneous equations.

$2x + 3y = 7$

$5x - 3y = 21$

Q2 Solve these simultaneous equations.

$5x + 3y = 19$

$5x - 2y = 4$

Q3 Solve these simultaneous equations.

$2x + 3y = 1$

$x - 2y = 11$

Q4 Two numbers have a sum of 13 and a difference of 3.
What are the two numbers?

Q5 Calculate the coordinates of the point of intersection of these lines.

$x + y = 8$

$y = 3x - 4$

The answers are given on pages 122–123.

21 Quadratic equations

Exam Questions and Answers

1 The diagram shows a square ABCD and a rectangle RBPQ.

$CP = 2$ cm and $RA = 3$ cm.

The length of the side of the square ABCD is x cm.

The rectangle RBPQ has an area of 42 cm^2.

Form an equation, in terms of x, for the area of the rectangle. Show that it can be written in the form $x^2 + 5x - 36 = 0$.

Solve $x^2 + 5x - 36 = 0$, and hence calculate the area of the square ABCD.

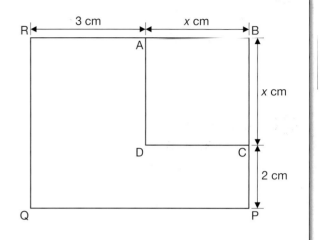

Answer

Area of RBPQ = $(3 + x)(x + 2)$
$(3 + x)(x + 2) = 42$
$3x + 6 + x^2 + 2x = 42$
$x^2 + 5x + 6 = 42$
$x^2 + 5x + 6 - 42 = 0$
$x^2 + 5x - 36 = 0$

$x^2 + 5x - 36 = 0$
$(x + 9)(x - 4) = 0$

$x + 9 = 0$ so $x = -9$
or $x - 4 = 0$ so $x = 4$

The side of the square is 4 cm (since you cannot have a length of –9 cm).

How to score full marks

● You are given that the rectangle RBPQ has an area of 42 cm^2 so find an algebraic equation for this, and solve it.

Area of rectangle = $(3 + x)(x + 2) = 42$

Start by expanding the brackets (remember FOIL), then simplify to get the form $x^2 + 5x - 36 = 0$ which is given in the question.

● Now solve this quadratic to produce two solutions of $x = -9$ and $x = 4$. As you cannot have a length of -9 cm, the length of the square is 4 cm.

● It is always a good idea to explain why you have rejected one of your solutions so that the examiner appreciates how clever you are.

Expanding quadratic expressions

You can use FOIL to remind you how to find the product of two binomial expressions.

F = First
O = Outsides
I = Insides
L = Last.

Product

F = First	$(x + 3)(2x - 5)$	$x \times 2x$	$= 2x^2$
O = Outsides	$(x + 3)(2x - 5)$	$x \times -5$	$= -5x$
I = Insides	$(x + 3)(2x - 5)$	$+3 \times 2x$	$= 6x$
L = Last	$(x + 3)(2x - 5)$	$+3 \times -5$	$= -15$

Factorising quadratic expressions

You can use the reverse process to write a quadratic expression as the product of two binomial expressions.

$$2x^2 + x - 15 = 2x^2 - 5x + 6x - 15$$
$$= x \times 2x - 5 \times x + 3 \times 2x - 3 \times 5$$
$$= x \times (2x - 5) + 3 \times (2x - 5)$$
$$= (2x - 5)(x + 3)$$

The difficult part of this method is working out how to rewrite the three terms as four terms, to find two brackets.

You need to work logically, using your common sense, to factorise quadratic expressions. You know that $2x^2 + x - 15 = (2x \quad)(x \quad)$ since $2x \times x = 2x^2$ as required.

Now you need to look for pairs of numbers that multiply together to give -15.

Factorising quadratic equations

Remember that if the product of two numbers is zero, then one or both of them must be zero.

If $ab = 0$ then either $a = 0$ or $b = 0$ or both $a = 0$ and $b = 0$.

You can use this fact to solve quadratic equations.

If $(2x - 5)(x + 3) = 0$ then either $(2x - 5) = 0$ or $(x + 3) = 0$ or both $(2x - 5) = 0$ and $(x + 3) = 0$.

If $(2x - 5) = 0$ then $x = \frac{5}{2}$ and if $(x + 3) = 0$ then $x = -3$.

Don't make these mistakes ...

Don't forget to give both solutions. Quadratic equations should always give you two solutions but:

- some quadratic equations cannot be solved e.g. $x^2 + x + 1 = 0$
- some quadratic equations give a repeated root e.g. $x^2 - 4x + 4 = 0$

You can factorise $x^2 - 4x + 4 = 0$ as $(x - 2)(x - 2) = 0$ to find the solutions $(x - 2) = 0$ or $(x - 2) = 0$, i.e. $x = 2$ (twice).

When you are asked to solve a quadratic equation you must always give both solutions.

Don't try to find the solutions by guesswork (trial and improvement).

Q1 Expand and simplify these expressions.

(a) $(x + 2)(x + 7)$ (b) $(3x - 2)(4x - 7)$

(c) $(2x - 1)^2$

Q2 Factorise these expressions completely.

(a) $x^2 + x - 12$ (b) $x^2 - x - 12$

(c) $x^2 + x - 3$

Q3 Solve the following quadratic equations.

(a) $(x - 4)(2x - 7) = 0$ (b) $x^2 - 7x + 12 = 0$

(c) $2x^2 - 5x - 3 = 0$ (d) $2x^2 - 5x = 3$

(e) $x^2 = 10x$

Q4 (a) Factorise $x^2 - 9x + 20$.

(b) Solve $x^2 + 2x = 0$.

Q5 Given that $(3x - 1)(x + 2) = 3x^2 + ax + b$, find a and b.

Q6 Expand $(a + b)(a - b)$ and use this to work out $1999^2 - 1998^2$ without using a calculator.

Q7 Simplify the expression $(x + 8)^2 - (x - 8)^2$.

Q8 The diagram shows a square ABCD with a triangle DCE, right-angled at D, placed so that the side DC is common.

The length of the side of the square is x cm and DE = 4 cm. The area of the whole figure ABCE is 48 cm^2.

(a) Show clearly that x satisfies the equation $x^2 + 2x = 48$.

(b) Solve the equation and write down the length of the side of the square.

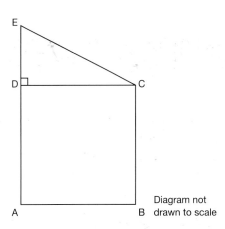

Diagram not drawn to scale

The answers are given on pages 123–124.

22 Further manipulation of equations

Exam Questions and Answers

1   Make g the subject of the following formula.

$$\frac{t(3 + g)}{8 - g} = 2$$

Answer

$$\frac{t(3 + g)}{8 - g} = 2$$

$$t(3 + g) = 2(8 - g)$$

$$3t + tg = 16 - 2g$$

$$tg = 16 - 2g - 3t$$

$$tg + 2g = 16 - 3t$$

$$g(t + 2) = 16 - 3t$$

$$g = \frac{16 - 3t}{t + 2}$$

How to score full marks

Use these steps to change the subject of the formula.

- First remove the fractions by multiplying both sides by $(8 - g)$.
- Expand the brackets.
- Subtract $3t$ from the left-hand side to get all terms in g on one side.
- Factorise, then divide both sides by $(t + 2)$ to make g the subject.

---

2   A cyclist travels 30 miles at an average speed of x miles per hour, followed by 20 miles at $(x + 5)$ miles per hour.

  (a)   Write down an expression, in terms of x, for the time taken, in hours, for the whole journey.

  The time taken for the whole journey is 3 hours.

  (b)   Write down an equation, in terms of x, for the time taken, in hours, for the whole journey and show that this simplifies to $3x^2 - 35x - 150 = 0$.

  (c)   Hence solve your equation to find the value of x.

Answer

(a) For first 30 miles: $T = \dfrac{30}{x}$

For next 20 miles: $T = \dfrac{20}{x+5}$

Total time $= \dfrac{30}{x} + \dfrac{20}{x+5}$

(b) $\dfrac{30}{x} + \dfrac{20}{x+5} = 3$

$30(x+5) + 20x = 3x(x+5)$
$30x + 150 + 20x = 3x^2 + 15x$
$3x^2 - 35x - 150 = 0$

(c) $3x^2 - 35x - 150 = 0$
$(3x + 10)(x - 15) = 0$
so $3x + 10 = 0$ or $x - 15 = 0$
$x = -\dfrac{10}{3}$ $x = 15$

The value of x is 15 (as x cannot be negative).

How to score full marks

- First, remember that $\text{speed} = \dfrac{\text{distance}}{\text{time}}$ and $\text{time} = \dfrac{\text{distance}}{\text{speed}}$.
  It is a good idea to write this down so the examiner knows what you are trying to do.

- Next, you need to break down the task by thinking about both parts of the journey separately.
  The total time for the whole journey is the sum of these two times.
  Remember that this is the solution to part (a) of the question.

- Given that the total time is 3 hours then $\dfrac{30}{x} + \dfrac{20}{x+5} = 3$.

- Remember that to solve questions involving algebraic fractions, you need to change all of the terms to fractions with the common denominator.

- You can put all of the terms over a common denominator of $x(x+5)$:
$$\dfrac{30}{x} = \dfrac{30(x+5)}{x(x+5)}$$
$$\dfrac{20}{x+5} = \dfrac{20x}{x(x+5)}$$
$$3 = \dfrac{3(x+5)}{x(x+5)}$$

- Now multiply throughout by $x(x+5)$:
$$30(x+5) + 20x = 3x(x+5)$$

- Expand the brackets and simplify to form the required quadratic equation.
$$3x^2 - 35x - 150 = 0$$

- Even if you can't prove the required quadratic equation, you can still gain marks for part (c) using the fact that the quadratic should simplify to $3x^2 - 35x - 150 = 0$.

  You can solve it to find the value of x.

- You should only give one value of x as the other is not suitable. It is always a good idea to check whether all of your solutions are valid.

Key points to remember

Rearranging formulae

At the Higher level you may be asked to rearrange formulae where the subject appears in more than one term. Most of these types of question can be solved using the following flow chart.

| Take out fractions by finding the common denominator and multiplying both sides by it. | → | Expand the brackets and take all terms that include the subject to one side. | → | Take the subject out, as a common factor, and divide both sides by the factor that multiplies it. |

The following example will help to illustrate this.

Make x the subject of the formula $p = \dfrac{xy}{x - y}$.

Take out the fractions by multiplying both sides by the denominator $(x - y)$.

$p(x - y) = xy$

Expand the brackets and take the subject to one side.

$px - py = xy$
$px = xy + py$
$px - xy = py$

Factorise terms containing the subject and divide both sides by the factor that multiplies it.

$x(p - y) = py$

$x = \dfrac{py}{p - y}$

Algebraic fractions

Remember how to work with numerical fractions. You can use the same methods to solve algebraic fractions.

To add or subtract fractions, change them all to equivalent fractions with a common denominator.

Common denominator

A common denominator is a number that can be divided exactly by all the denominators of the fractions you are working with.

Don't make these mistakes ...

Don't try to add or subtract algebraic fractions unless they have common denominators.

Don't despair! You can always find a common denominator by multiplying the denominators together.

So $\dfrac{1}{x + 1}$, $\dfrac{1}{x + 2}$ and $\dfrac{1}{2x + 1}$ will have a common denominator of $(x + 1)(x + 2)(2x + 1)$. Phew!!

Q1 Make y the subject of the formula $q = \dfrac{xy}{x-y}$.

Q2 A formula states $s = \dfrac{1-t^2}{1+t^2}$.

(a) Find the value of s when $t = \frac{1}{3}$.

(b) Rearrange the formula to make t the subject.

Q3 Rearrange the formula $p = \sqrt{\dfrac{s}{s-t}}$ to make s the subject.

Q4 Simplify fully the expression $\dfrac{7x+21}{2x^2+5x-3}$.

Q5 The expression $x^2 - 10x + 14 + a$, where a is an integer, can be written in the form $(x-b)^2$, where b is an integer.
Calculate the values of a and b.

Q6 Write as a single fraction $\dfrac{1}{x-2} + \dfrac{1}{x+3}$.

Q7 Solve the following equation.
$$\dfrac{3}{x+2} - \dfrac{2}{2x-3} = \dfrac{1}{7}$$

The answers are given on pages 125–126.

HIGHER TIER
H

Exam Questions and Answers

---

1 Solve the equation $3x^2 + 2x - 7 = 0$, giving your answers to 2 decimal places.

Answer

$a = 3$, $b = 2$, $c = -7$.

$$x = \frac{-2 \pm \sqrt{2^2 - 4 \times 3 \times -7}}{2 \times 3}$$

$$= \frac{-2 \pm \sqrt{88}}{6}$$

$$x = \frac{-2 + 9.380\,831\,52}{6}$$

$$\text{or } x = \frac{-2 - 9.380\,831\,52}{6}$$

$x = 1.230\,138\,587$ or $-1.896\,805\,253$
$x = 1.23$ (2 d.p.) or $x = -1.90$ (2 d.p.)

How to score full marks

- The question says 'give your answer correct to 2 decimal places'. This is usually a hint to use the formula.
- Comparing $3x^2 + 2x - 7 = 0$, with the general form $ax^2 + bx + c = 0$:

  $a = 3$, $b = 2$, $c = -7$.

- Substitute these values in the formula $x = \dfrac{-b \pm \sqrt{b^2 - 4ac}}{2a}$.

- Be careful when you round $-1.896\,805\,253$ to two decimal places.

---

2 (a) (i) Factorise $4x^2 - 37x + 9$.

(ii) Hence, or otherwise, solve the equation $4x^2 - 37x + 9 = 0$.

(b) By considering your answers to part (a), find all the solutions of the equation
$4y^4 - 37y^2 + 9 = 0$.

Answer

(a) (i) $4x^2 - 37x + 9$
$= (4x - 1)(x - 9)$

(ii) $(4x - 1)(x - 9) = 0$
$(4x - 1) = 0$ so $x = \frac{1}{4}$ or
$(x - 9) = 0$ so $x = 9$

(b) As $x = y^2$, solutions will be
$y^2 = \frac{1}{4}$ so $y = \pm\frac{1}{2}$
and $y^2 = 9$ so $y = \pm 3$

How to score full marks

- Use what you know:

  $4x^2 - 37x + 9 = (2x \quad)(2x \quad)$ (as $2x \times 2x = 4x^2$)
  or $4x^2 - 37x + 9 = (4x \quad)(x \quad)$ (as $4x \times x = 4x^2$)

- If $4x^2 - 37x + 9 = 0$ then $(4x - 1)(x - 9) = 0$

  so $(4x - 1) = 0$ or $(x - 9) = 0$
  $x = \frac{1}{4}$ or $x = 9$

- Compare $4x^2 - 37x + 9 = 0$

  with $4y^4 - 37y^2 + 9 = 0$

- You should notice that if you substitute $x = y^2$ into the second equation, you find the equation you have already solved.

  Then the solutions will be:

  $y^2 = \frac{1}{4}$ and $y^2 = 9$

- Take square roots, and remember that there are two solutions in each case.

  $y = \pm\frac{1}{2}$ and $y = \pm 3$

Key points to remember

Definition: A quadratic equation has the form $ax^2 + bx + c = 0$ where a, b and c are rational numbers.

$2x^2 + x - 15 = 0$ is a quadratic equation with $a = 2$, $b = 1$ and $c = -15$.

Factorising quadratic equations (1)

Remember that if the product of the two numbers is zero then one or both of them must be zero.

If $ab = 0$ then either $a = 0$ or $b = 0$ or both $a = 0$ and $b = 0$.

You can use this important fact to solve quadratic equations.

If $(2x - 5)(x + 3) = 0$ then either $(2x - 5) = 0$ or $(x + 3) = 0$ or both $(2x - 5) = 0$ and $(x + 3) = 0$.

Note: If $(2x - 5) = 0$ then $x = \frac{5}{2}$ and if $(x + 3) = 0$ then $x = -3$.

So the solutions of $(2x - 5)(x + 3) = 0$ are $x = \frac{5}{2}$ and $x = -3$.

Factorising quadratic equations (2)

At the Higher tier, not all quadratic equations can be solved using the method described above. You will need to be able to solve quadratics by using the formula and by iteration techniques. In the exam, the question should make it clear which method you should use. If it doesn't, you can use any method you like.

Quadratic equations – solution by formula

If you can't see how to factorise a quadratic, you can use the formula.

For any quadratic of the form $ax^2 + bx + c = 0$:

$$x = \frac{-b \pm \sqrt{b^2 - 4ac}}{2a}$$

Note: The formula for solving quadratic equations will be given in the exam, so you don't need to remember it – but you do need to know how to use it correctly.

Don't make these mistakes ...

Don't forget that quadratic equations should always give you two solutions but:

- some quadratic equations cannot be solved e.g. $x^2 + x + 1 = 0$
- some quadratic equations give a repeated root e.g. $x^2 - 4x + 4 = 0$

  $x^2 - 4x + 4 = 0$
  can be factorised as $(x - 2)(x - 2) = 0$
  with solutions $(x - 2) = 0$ or $(x - 2) = 0$
  i.e. $x = 2$ (twice)

- whenever you are asked to solve a quadratic equation you must give both solutions.

Don't forget that the formula $x = \dfrac{-b \pm \sqrt{b^2 - 4ac}}{2a}$ is a short way of writing two different solutions:

$$x = \frac{-b + \sqrt{b^2 - 4ac}}{2a} \quad \text{and} \quad x = \frac{-b - \sqrt{b^2 - 4ac}}{2a}$$

Remember that the whole of the numerator is divided by $2a$.

The $\sqrt{b^2 - 4ac}$ of the formula is very important. It is called the discriminant.

If $\sqrt{b^2 - 4ac} = 0$ then the equation has only one (repeated) root.

If $\sqrt{b^2 - 4ac} < 0$ then the equation has no roots.

If $\sqrt{b^2 - 4ac}$ is a square number, the quadratic can be solved by factorising (which is almost always easier than using the formula).

Never, ever try to find the solutions of a quadratic equation by guesswork (trial and improvement) unless you are told to do so.

Q1 Solve the equation $2x^2 + 7x = 4$.

Q2 Solve the equation $3x^2 - 2x = 0$.

Q3 Solve the equation $\dfrac{2}{x + 2} = \dfrac{x - 1}{x}$.

Q4 Write $x^2 + 4x - 9$ in the form $(x + a)^2 - b$.
Hence solve the equation $x^2 + 4x - 9 = 0$, giving your answer in the form $x = a \pm \sqrt{b}$.

Q5 Solve $x^2 - 2x - 1 = 0$, giving your answers correct to 2 d.p.

Q6 (a) Factorise $3x^2 - 2x - 8$.

(b) Solve the equation $3x^2 - 2x - 8 = 0$.

(c) Hence write down all the integers which satisfy $3x^2 - 2x - 8 \leqslant 0$.

The answers are given on pages 126–127.

Chapter 1 Transformations

Answer	How to solve these questions

Q1 (a) See the diagram opposite.

(a)

(b) (i) The transformation of A onto B is an enlargement, scale factor 2, centre of enlargement (0, 0).
(ii) The transformation of A onto C is a rotation, 90° clockwise, centre of rotation (3, 2).

(b) (i) The transformation is an enlargement, so you must give the scale factor (2) and the centre of enlargement (0, 0).

(ii) The transformation is a rotation, so you must give the angle (90°), the direction (clockwise) and the centre of rotation (3, 2).

Q2 (a) See the diagram opposite.
(b) See the diagram opposite.

(a)   **(b)**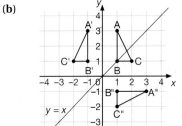

(c) Rotation of 90° anticlockwise about the origin.

(c) The question asks for a single transformation, and this is a rotation of 90° anticlockwise (or counterclockwise), centre of rotation (0, 0), or the origin.

Q3 **(a)** See the diagram opposite.

(a)

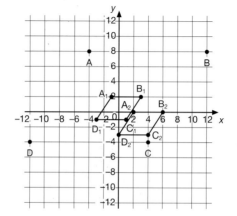

(b) **(i)** Area of A = 12 square units

(ii) Area of enlargement = 48 square units

(iii) 1 : 4

(b) **(i)** You can either count the squares or use the formula (remember to state the units).

(ii) Again, you can count the squares or use the formula (remember to state the units).

(iii) Ratio = 12 : 48 = 1 : 4 (cancelling down)

Q4 See the diagram opposite.
Coordinates of the points:
$A_2 = (2, 0)$
$B_2 = (6, 0)$
$C_2 = (4, -3)$
$D_2 = (0, -3)$

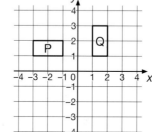

Q5 **(a)** See the diagram opposite.
(b) See the diagram opposite.

(a)

(b)

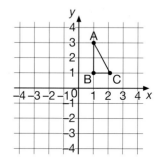

(c) Translation through vector $\begin{pmatrix} 5 \\ 2 \end{pmatrix}$.

(c) The single transformation is a translation. You should describe it fully, as a translation through vector $\begin{pmatrix} 5 \\ 2 \end{pmatrix}$.

Answer	How to solve these questions

Q1 (a) AC = 10.3 m (1 d.p.)

(a) $AC^2 = AB^2 + BC^2$
$AC^2 = 8.3^2 + 6.1^2$
$AC^2 = 68.89 + 37.21$
$AC^2 = 106.1$
$AC = \sqrt{106.1}$
$AC = 10.300\,485\,43$
$AC = 10.3$ m (1 d.p.)

Remember to include the units in the answer and round off to an appropriate degree of accuracy (1 decimal place seems reasonable here).

(b) AD = 6.6 m (1 d.p.)

(b) $AB^2 = AD^2 + DB^2$
$8.3^2 = AD^2 + 5.0^2$
$68.89 = AD^2 + 25.0$
$AD^2 = 68.89 - 25.0$
$AD^2 = 43.89$
$AD = \sqrt{43.89}$
$AD = 6.624\,952\,83$
$AD = 6.6$ m (1 d.p.)

Remember to include the units in the answer and round off to an appropriate degree of accuracy (1 decimal place seems reasonable here).

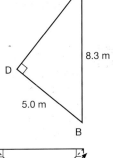

Q2 The length of a diagonal $= \sqrt{200}$ cm

Using Pythagoras' theorem:
$x^2 = 10^2 + 10^2$
$x^2 = 100 + 100$
$x^2 = 200$
$x = \sqrt{200}$ (leaving in surd form)
The length of a diagonal $= \sqrt{200}$ cm

Q3 Height $= \sqrt{84}$ cm

To find the height, you can split the isosceles triangle into two right-angled triangles.
Use Pythagoras' theorem: $a^2 + b^2 = c^2$
$4^2 + h^2 = 10^2$
$16 + h^2 = 100$
$h^2 = 100 - 16$
$h^2 = 84$
$h = \sqrt{84}$ (leaving in surd form)

Height $= \sqrt{84}$ cm

Q4 (a) Area = 28 cm^2

(a) Area of the parallelogram = base × perpendicular height
$= (2 + 5) \times 4$
$= 28$ cm^2

(b) Perimeter = 22.9 cm (1 d.p.)

(b) To work out the perimeter, you need to find the length of the slant height.
$x^2 = 4^2 + 2^2$
$x^2 = 16 + 4$
$x^2 = 20$
$x = \sqrt{20}$
$x = 4.472\,135\,955$

Perimeter $= 7 + 4.472\,135\,955 + 7 + 4.472\,135\,955$
$= 22.944\,271\,91$
$= 22.9$ cm (1 d.p.)

Q5 $h = 2.08\,\text{m}$ (2 d.p.)

Since the triangle is right-angled, and you know two sides, then you can use Pythagoras' theorem to find the third side.

The length of the hypotenuse is given, so use:

$$2.75^2 = h^2 + 1.80^2$$
$$7.5625 = h^2 + 3.24$$
$$h^2 = 7.5625 - 3.24$$
$$h^2 = 4.3225$$
$$h = 2.079\,062\,289$$
$$h = 2.08\,\text{m}\ (2\,\text{d.p.})$$

It is reasonable to correct the answer to two decimal places, as this is how the original numbers were given.

Q6 $AB = \sqrt{13}$ units

$BC = \sqrt{65}$ units

$CA = 2\sqrt{13}$ units

ABC is a right-angled triangle as $CA^2 + AB^2 = BC^2$

$$AB^2 = 2^2 + 3^2$$
$$AB^2 = 4 + 9$$
$$AB = \sqrt{13}\ \text{units}$$
$$BC^2 = 7^2 + 4^2$$
$$BC^2 = 49 + 16$$
$$BC = \sqrt{65}\ \text{units}$$
$$AC^2 = 6^2 + 4^2$$
$$AC^2 = 36 + 16$$
$$AC = \sqrt{52}\ \text{units}$$

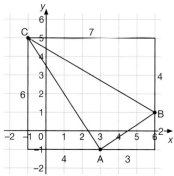

Hint: In examples like these it is usually better to leave the answers in surd (square root) form.

If ABC is a right-angled triangle then the square on the hypotenuse must be equal to the sum of the squares on the other two sides. (Pythagoras' theorem is true for all right-angled triangles.)

You need to show that $BC^2 = AC^2 + AB^2$

$$LHS = BC^2 = (\sqrt{65})^2 = 65$$
$$RHS = AC^2 + AB^2 = (\sqrt{52})^2 + (\sqrt{13})^2 \quad \text{as } (\sqrt{52})^2 = 52 \text{ and } (\sqrt{13})^2 = 13$$
$$= 52 + 13 = 65$$

As they are the same, this shows that the triangle ABC is right-angled.

Chapter 3 Angle and tangent properties of circles

Q1 (a) Angle $ABC = 34°$

(a) $\angle ACB = 90°$ (as the angle in a semicircle is always 90°)
$\angle ABC = 180° - 90° - 56°$
$= 34°$ (as the angles in triangle ABC total 180°)

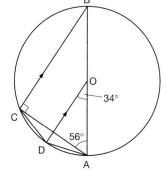

(b) Angle $AOD = 34°$

(b) $\angle AOD = 34°$ (as corresponding angles between parallel lines OD and BC are equal, $\angle AOD = \angle ABC$)

(c) Angle $ACD = 17°$

(c) $\angle ACD = 17°$ (as the angle subtended by arc/chord AD at the centre is twice that subtended at the circumference)

(d) Angle $OAD = 73°$

(d) $\angle ODA = \angle AOD$ (base angles of isosceles triangle)
$\angle ODA + \angle AOD = 180° - 34°$ (angle sum of triangle)
$\angle ODA + \angle AOD = 146°$
$\angle ODA = 73°$

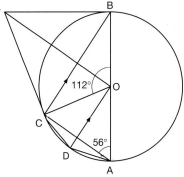

(e) Angle BOT = 56°

(e) ∠BOC = 112° (as the angle subtended by arc/chord BC at the centre is twice that subtended at the circumference)

∠BOT = $\frac{1}{2}$ × 112° (as ∠COT = ∠BOT by the tangent properties of a circle)

∠BOT = 56°

Q2 (a) ∠POQ = 75°

(a) ∠POQ = 75° (∠POQ = ∠POR as triangles POQ and POR are congruent triangles)

(b) ∠OPQ = 15°

(b) ∠OQP = 90° (as the tangent to a circle is perpendicular to the radius at the point of contact)

∠OPQ = 15° (as the angles of triangle OPQ total 180°)

(c) ∠OPR = 15°

(c) ∠OPR = 15° (∠OPR = ∠OPQ as triangles POR and POQ are congruent triangles)

Q3 Angle POQ = 130°

∠CRO = ∠CQO = 90° (as the tangent to a circle is perpendicular to the radius at the point of contact)

∠RCO = ∠QCO = 20° (∠RCO = ∠QCO as the triangle RCO and triangle QCO are congruent triangles)

∠ROC = 70° (angle sum of triangle ROC)

∠QOC = 70° (angle sum of triangle QOC)

∠ROQ = 140° (∠ROQ = ∠ROC + ∠QOC)

∠ROP = 90° (as the interior angles between parallel lines CA and OP are supplementary and add up to 180°)

∠POQ = 130° (as the angles in a circle add up to 360°)

Q4 The length of the chord is $2\sqrt{20}$ cm.

Let O be the centre of the circle and OX the perpendicular bisector of the chord.

Use Pythagoras' theorem in the right-angled triangle OAX.

$6^2 = 4^2 + AX^2$
$AX^2 = 36 - 16$
$AX^2 = 20$
$AX = \sqrt{20}$
$AB = 2 \times AX = 2 \times \sqrt{20}$
$AB = 2 \times \sqrt{20}$ cm
$AB = 2\sqrt{20}$ cm

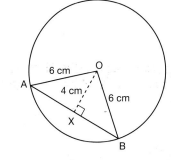

Q5 The distance between the chords is 27.9 cm (3 s.f.).

Use Pythagoras' theorem in the right-angled triangle ORY.

$15^2 = 6^2 + OY^2$
$225 = 36 + OY^2$
$OY^2 = 189$
$OY = 13.747\,727\,08$

How to solve these questions

Now use Pythagoras' theorem in the right-angled triangle OPX.

$$15^2 = 5^2 + OX^2$$
$$225 = 25 + OX^2$$
$$OX^2 = 200$$
$$OX = 14.142\,135\,62$$

The distance between the two chords = OY + OX.

$$OY + OX = 13.747\,727\,08 + 14.142\,135$$
$$= 27.889\,862\,071$$
$$= 27.9\,\text{cm (3 s.f.)}$$

Chapter 4 Sine, cosine, tangent

Answer

How to solve these questions

Q1 Area of parallelogram = 37.2 cm² (3 s.f.)

First you need to find the height of the parallelogram.

The identified sides are 'opposite' and 'hypotenuse' so use:

$$\text{sine } x = \frac{\text{opposite}}{\text{hypotenuse}}$$

$$\sin 48° = \frac{h}{5}$$

$$h = 5 \times \sin 48°$$
$$h = 5 \times 0.7431$$
$$h = 3.7155$$

Area of parallelogram = base × perpendicular height
$$= 10 \times 3.7155 = 37.155 = 37.2\,\text{cm}^2 \text{ (3 s.f.)}$$

Q2 The required angle is 28.6° (3 s.f.).

The identified sides are 'adjacent' and 'opposite' so use:

$$\text{tangent } x = \frac{\text{opposite}}{\text{adjacent}}$$

$$\tan x = \frac{6}{11}$$

$$x = \tan^{-1} \frac{6}{11}$$

$$x = 28.610\,459\,67°$$
$$x = 28.6° \text{ (3 s.f.)}$$

Q3 Distance north = 2.18 km (3 s.f.)

Take PS as the distance north.

$$\cos 85° = \frac{PS}{25}$$

$$PS = 25 \times \cos 85°$$
$$PS = 2.178\,893\,569\,\text{km}$$
Distance north = 2.18 km (3 s.f.)

Distance east = 24.9 km (3 s.f.)

Take SR as the distance east.

$$\sin 85° = \frac{SR}{25}$$

$$SR = 25 \times \sin 85°$$
$$SR = 24.904\,867\,45\,\text{km}$$
Distance east = 24.9 km (3 s.f.)

Q4 **(a)** The distance of A from B = 6.24 km (3 s.f.)

(a) You can use Pythagoras' theorem to calculate the third side.

$$8^2 = AB^2 + 5^2$$
$$64 = AB^2 + 25$$
$$AB^2 = 64 - 25$$
$$AB^2 = 39$$
$$AB = 6.244\,997\,998\text{ km}$$
$$AB = 6.24\text{ km (3 s.f.)}$$

(b) **(i)** $x = 51.3°$ (1 d.p.)

(b) **(i)** $\cos x = \frac{5}{8}$

$$x = \cos^{-1}\frac{5}{8}$$
$$x = 51.317\,812\,55°$$
$$x = 51.3°\text{ (1 d.p.)}$$

(ii) Bearing = 321.3° (1 d.p.)

(ii) Bearing
$$= 270° + 51.317\,812\,55°$$
$$= 321.317\,812\,6°$$
$$= 321.3°\text{ (1 d.p.)}$$

(iii) Bearing = 141.3° (1 d.p.)

(iii) $\angle BAC$
$$= 90° - 51.317\,812\,55°$$
$$= 38.682\,187\,45°$$
Bearing
$$= 180° - 38.682\,187\,45°$$
$$= 141.317\,812\,5°$$
$$= 141.3°\text{ (1 d.p.)}$$

$90° - 51.3...°$ (angles of a triangle add up to 180°)

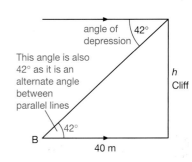

Q5 **(a)** Height of the cliff = 36.0 m (3 s.f.)

(a) $\tan 42° = \dfrac{h}{40}$
$$h = 40 \times \tan 42°$$
$$h = 36.016\,161\,77\text{ m}$$
$$h = 36.0\text{ m (3 s.f.)}$$

This angle is also 42° as it is an alternate angle between parallel lines

(b) Angle of elevation = 7.08° (3 s.f.)

(b) $\tan\theta = \dfrac{36.016\,161\,77}{290}$

$$\theta = \tan^{-1}\frac{36.016\,161\,77}{290}$$

$$\theta = 7.079\,522\,804°$$
$$\theta = 7.08°\text{ (3 s.f.)}$$

95

Answer	**How to solve these questions**

Q1 $\cos A = -0.5$

So angle A is obtuse.

$A = 120°$

Draw a sketch so you can see what the question requires.

You are given three sides and have to find an angle, so you can use the cosine rule.

$$\cos A = \frac{b^2 + c^2 - a^2}{2bc}$$

Remember that the largest angle is always opposite the longest side.

$$\cos A = \frac{1.5^2 + 2.5^2 - 3.5^2}{2 \times 1.5 \times 2.5}$$

$$\cos A = \frac{2.25 + 6.25 - 12.25}{7.5} = \frac{-3.75}{7.5}$$

If the cosine of an angle is negative, the angle is obtuse, since the cosine of an obtuse angle is negative!

$$\cos A = -0.5$$
$$A = 120°$$

You are given three sides and have to find an angle, so you can use the cosine rule.

Q2 Angle ABC = 101.4° (1 d.p.)

$$\cos ABC = \frac{a^2 + c^2 - b^2}{2ac}$$

$$\cos ABC = \frac{3.1^2 + 8.6^2 - 9.7^2}{2 \times 3.1 \times 8.6}$$

$$\cos ABC = \frac{-10.52}{53.32}$$

$$\cos ABC = -0.197\,299\,324$$

The negative value means that angle ABC is obtuse.

$$\angle ABC = 101.379\,075\,2°$$
$$\angle ABC = 101.4° \text{ (1 d.p.)}$$

Q3 Distance = 26.3 km (3 s.f.)

Bearing = 046° (to the nearest whole degree)

Draw a sketch so you can see what the question requires.

From the sketch, the distance is represented by the line AC and the bearing is 32° + ∠BAC.

Add the details of the angles of triangle ABC to the sketch.

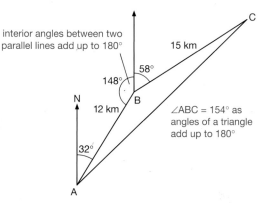

Now use the cosine rule on triangle ABC.

$$b^2 = a^2 + c^2 - 2ac\cos B$$
$$AC^2 = 15^2 + 12^2 - (2 \times 15 \times 12 \times \cos 154°)$$
$$AC^2 = 369 - (-323.565\,856\,7)$$
$$AC^2 = 369 + 323.565\,856\,7$$
$$AC^2 - 692.565\,856\,7$$
$$AC = 26.316\,646$$

So the distance = 26.3 km (3 s.f.).

The bearing is $32° + \angle BAC$.

Use the sine rule to find angle BAC.

$$\frac{\sin A}{a} = \frac{\sin B}{b}$$

$$\frac{\sin BAC}{BC} = \frac{\sin ABC}{AC}$$

Substitute the given values, using the unrounded value for AC.

$$\frac{\sin BAC}{15} = \frac{\sin 154°}{26.316\,646}$$

$$\sin BAC = \frac{15 \times \sin 154°}{26.316\,646}$$

$$\sin BAC = 0.249\,863\,421$$

$$\angle BAC = 14.469\,430\,3°$$

The bearing = $32° + \angle BAC$
$$= 32° + 14.469\,430\,3°$$
$$= 46.469\,430\,3°$$
$$= 046° \text{ (to the nearest whole degree)}$$

Q4 **(a)** AB = 9.51 km (3 s.f.)

(a) Draw a sketch, including details of the angles of $\triangle APB$.

$\angle APB = 80°$

Now you can use the cosine rule on the triangle ABP.

$$p^2 = a^2 + b^2 - 2ab\cos P$$
$$AB^2 = 4.5^2 + 9.2^2 -$$
$$(2 \times 4.5 \times 9.2 \times \cos 80°)$$
$$AB^2 = 104.89 - (14.378\,069\,11)$$
$$AB^2 = 90.511\,930\,89$$
$$AB = 9.513\,775\,848$$

So the distance AB = 9.51 km (3 s.f.).

$\angle APB = 80° (= 117° - 37°)$

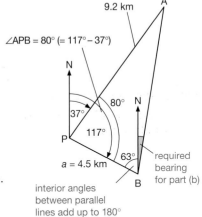

9.2 km A

N 80° N

37°

117°

P

63° required bearing for part (b)

a = 4.5 km

B

interior angles between parallel lines add up to 180°

(b) Bearing of A from ship B = 009° (to the nearest whole degree)

(b) Now use the sine rule to find angle PBA.

$$\frac{\sin P}{p} = \frac{\sin B}{b}$$

$$\frac{\sin 80°}{9.513\,775\,848} = \frac{\sin B}{9.2}$$

$$\sin B = \frac{9.2 \times \sin 80°}{9.513\,775\,848}$$

$$\sin B = 0.952\,327\,6$$

$$B = 72.237\,187\,27°$$

The bearing = $\angle PBA - 63°$
$$= 72.237\,187\,27° - 63°$$
$$= 9.237\,187\,275°$$
$$= 009° \text{ (to the nearest whole degree)}$$

Q5 AC = 6.05 cm (3 s.f.)

∠BAD = 55° (as the angles of the triangle BAD add up to 180°)

∠ADC = 75° (as the angles on a straight line add up to 180°)

Use the sine rule to find BD.

$$\frac{BD}{\sin BAD} = \frac{AB}{\sin ADB}$$

$$\frac{BD}{\sin 55°} = \frac{8.3}{\sin 105°}$$

$$BD = \frac{8.3 \times \sin 55°}{\sin 105°}$$

BD = 7.038 803 377
BC = BD + DC
BC = 13.138 803 38

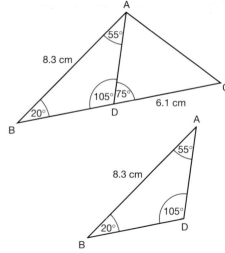

Use the cosine rule on the triangle ABC.

$$b^2 = a^2 + c^2 - 2ac\cos B$$

AC² = 13.138 803 38² + 8.3² −
(2 × 13.138 803 38 × 8.3 × cos 20°)
AC² = 241.518 154 3 − (204.950 847 3)
AC² = 36.567 306 91
AC = 6.047 090 78

So the distance AC = 6.05 cm (3 s.f.).

Chapter 6 Vectors

Q1 (a) $\mathbf{p} + \mathbf{q} = \begin{pmatrix} 7 \\ 1 \end{pmatrix}$

(b) $2\mathbf{p} - 3\mathbf{q} = \begin{pmatrix} 4 \\ 17 \end{pmatrix}$

(c) $|\mathbf{p} + \mathbf{q}| = \sqrt{50}$

(a) $\mathbf{p} + \mathbf{q} = \begin{pmatrix} 5 \\ 4 \end{pmatrix} + \begin{pmatrix} 2 \\ -3 \end{pmatrix} = \begin{pmatrix} 7 \\ 1 \end{pmatrix}$

(b) $2\mathbf{p} - 3\mathbf{q} = 2 \times \begin{pmatrix} 5 \\ 4 \end{pmatrix} - 3 \times \begin{pmatrix} 2 \\ -3 \end{pmatrix} = \begin{pmatrix} 10 \\ 8 \end{pmatrix} - \begin{pmatrix} 6 \\ -9 \end{pmatrix} = \begin{pmatrix} 10-6 \\ 8--9 \end{pmatrix}$

$= \begin{pmatrix} 4 \\ 17 \end{pmatrix}$

(c) $|\mathbf{p} + \mathbf{q}| = \sqrt{7^2 + 1^2}$
$= \sqrt{50}$

Q2 (a) $\overrightarrow{PT} = \mathbf{a}$
(b) $\overrightarrow{PR} = \mathbf{b} + \mathbf{a}$

(c) $\overrightarrow{RT} = -\mathbf{b}$
(d) $\overrightarrow{SR} = \frac{3}{2}\mathbf{b}$

(e) $\overrightarrow{PS} = \mathbf{a} - \frac{1}{2}\mathbf{b}$

(a) $\overrightarrow{PT} = \mathbf{a}$　　　　(as PT is parallel to QR and the same length)

(b) $\overrightarrow{PR} = \overrightarrow{PQ} + \overrightarrow{QR}$
$= \mathbf{b} + \mathbf{a}$

(c) $\overrightarrow{RT} = -\mathbf{b}$　　　　(as RT is parallel to QP and the same length)

(d) $\overrightarrow{SR} = \overrightarrow{ST} + \overrightarrow{TR}$
$= \frac{1}{2}\overrightarrow{TR} + \overrightarrow{TR} = \frac{3}{2}\overrightarrow{TR}$　(as TR is twice the length of ST)
$= \frac{3}{2}\mathbf{b}$

(e) $\overrightarrow{PS} = \overrightarrow{PT} + \overrightarrow{TS}$
$= \overrightarrow{PT} + \frac{1}{2}\overrightarrow{RT}$　　　　(as TR is twice the length of ST)
$= \mathbf{a} + \frac{1}{2}(-\mathbf{b})$
$= \mathbf{a} - \frac{1}{2}\mathbf{b}$

Q3 **(a)** See the diagram opposite.

(a)

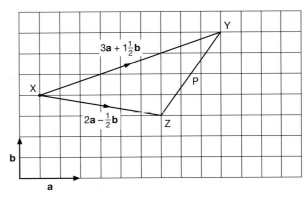

(b) $\overrightarrow{XP} = 2\frac{1}{2}\mathbf{a} + \frac{1}{2}\mathbf{b}$

(b) $\overrightarrow{XP} = \overrightarrow{XZ} + \frac{1}{2}\overrightarrow{ZY}$

$= 2\mathbf{a} - \frac{1}{2}\mathbf{b} + \frac{1}{2}(\overrightarrow{ZX} + \overrightarrow{XY})$

$= 2\mathbf{a} - \frac{1}{2}\mathbf{b} + \frac{1}{2}(-2\mathbf{a} + \frac{1}{2}\mathbf{b} + 3\mathbf{a} + 1\frac{1}{2}\mathbf{b})$

$= 2\mathbf{a} - \frac{1}{2}\mathbf{b} - \mathbf{a} + \frac{1}{4}\mathbf{b} + 1\frac{1}{2}\mathbf{a} + \frac{3}{4}\mathbf{b}$

$= 2\frac{1}{2}\mathbf{a} + \frac{1}{2}\mathbf{b}$

Note that since you are told that you '**must** show all your working' then it is important to calculate the above rather than find it from the grid.

Q4 $\overrightarrow{XY} = \overrightarrow{XP} + \overrightarrow{PY}$
$XY = \mathbf{a} + \mathbf{b}$
But $\overrightarrow{QX} = \overrightarrow{XP}$
and $\overrightarrow{YR} = \overrightarrow{PY}$
$\overrightarrow{QR} = \overrightarrow{QP} + \overrightarrow{PR}$
$\overrightarrow{QR} = 2\mathbf{a} + 2\mathbf{b}$
$\overrightarrow{QR} = 2(\mathbf{a} + \mathbf{b})$
$\overrightarrow{QR} = 2\overrightarrow{XY}$

The magnitude of $\overrightarrow{QR}$ is twice the magnitude of $\overrightarrow{XY}$ so the length QR = 2XY.
As $\overrightarrow{QR}$ is a multiple of $\overrightarrow{XY}$, $\overrightarrow{QR}$ and $\overrightarrow{XY}$ are in the same direction and therefore are parallel.

From the diagram:
$\overrightarrow{XY} = \overrightarrow{XP} + \overrightarrow{PY}$
$\overrightarrow{XY} = \mathbf{a} + \mathbf{b}$
As X is the midpoint of QP then QX = XP
and similarly as Y is the midpoint of PR then YR = PY.
From the diagram:
$\overrightarrow{QR} = \overrightarrow{QP} + \overrightarrow{PR}$
$\overrightarrow{QR} = 2\mathbf{a} + 2\mathbf{b}$
$\overrightarrow{QR} = 2(\mathbf{a} + \mathbf{b})$
$\overrightarrow{QR} = 2\overrightarrow{XY}$

It is important to give reasons for your conclusions.
● Since the magnitude of $\overrightarrow{QR}$ is twice the magnitude of XY then the length QR = 2XY.
● Similarly $\overrightarrow{QR}$ is a multiple of $\overrightarrow{XY}$ so $\overrightarrow{QR}$ and $\overrightarrow{XY}$ are in the same direction and parallel.

Q5 **(a)** $\overrightarrow{AC} = \mathbf{a} + \mathbf{b}$
(b) $\overrightarrow{AO} = \mathbf{b}$
(c) $\overrightarrow{OB} = \mathbf{a} - \mathbf{b}$
(d) $\overrightarrow{AD} = 2\mathbf{b}$
$\overrightarrow{AC} = \mathbf{a} + \mathbf{b}$ and $\overrightarrow{FD} = \mathbf{a} + \mathbf{b}$
$\overrightarrow{AF} = \mathbf{b} - \mathbf{a}$ and $\overrightarrow{CD} = \mathbf{b} - \mathbf{a}$
AC is parallel and equal to FD.
AF is parallel and equal to CD.
Therefore ACDF is a parallelogram.

(a) $\overrightarrow{AC} = \overrightarrow{AB} + \overrightarrow{BC} = \mathbf{a} + \mathbf{b}$
(b) $\overrightarrow{AO} = \mathbf{b}$
(c) $\overrightarrow{OB} = \overrightarrow{OA} + \overrightarrow{AB} = -\mathbf{b} + \mathbf{a} = \mathbf{a} - \mathbf{b}$
(d) You must show your working and your reasons.

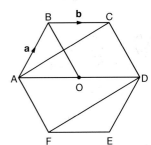

| **Answer** | | **How to solve these questions** |

Q1 $6 \times 2^4 = 6 \times 2 \times 2 \times 2 \times 2$
$= 96$

A common error here is to say $6 \times 2^4 = 12^4$ ✗

You must calculate 6×2^4 as $6 \times (2 \times 2 \times 2 \times 2) = 6 \times 16 = 96$

Q2 See next column.

+	1^2	2^2	3^2	4^2	5^2	6^2
1^2	2	5	10	17	26	37
2^2	5	8	13	20	29	40
3^2	10	13	18	25	34	45
4^2	17	20	25	32	41	52
5^2	26	29	34	41	50	61
6^2	37	40	45	52	61	72

Q3 (i) $2.021\,22 \times 10^{-6}$

(ii) $6.295\,302\,013 \times 10^{-11}$

You will be allowed to use a calculator for these questions, so practise keying in standard form numbers (use the EXP or EE keys).

| 2.02122 -6 | | 2.02122 -6 |
| 6.295302013 -11 | or | 6.295302013 -11 |

Remember to write the results out in proper standard form.
It is always a good idea to check your answer by approximating.

Q4 (i) $pq = (6 \times 10^{-2}) \times (3 \times 10^{-4})$
$= 6 \times 10^{-2} \times 3 \times 10^{-4}$
$= 6 \times 3 \times 10^{-2} \times 10^{-4}$
$= 18 \times 10^{-2-4}$
$= 18 \times 10^{-6}$
$= 1.8 \times 10^1 \times 10^{-6}$
$= 1.8 \times 10^{1-6}$
$= 1.8 \times 10^{-5}$

(i) Remember that pq means $p \times q$.
You can use the laws of indices ($a^m \times a^n = a^{m+n}$) to multiply 10^{-2} and 10^{-4}.
Remember that 18×10^{-6} is not in standard form.
You can use the fact that $18 = 1.8 \times 10$ or 1.8×10^1, with the laws of indices again, to find the correct answer.

(ii) $p - q = (6 \times 10^{-2}) - (3 \times 10^{-4})$
$= 0.06 - 0.0003$
$= 0.0597$
$= 5.97 \times 10^{-2}$

(ii) Remember that numbers in standard form can only be added or subtracted if the power of 10 is the same in both of them.
Here it is best to convert the numbers to ordinary form and then subtract.
The answer can be given in standard form or left as 0.0597.
In this case, the question does not say which form to use, but you should always check.

Q5 8 minutes (to the nearest minute)

Remember that time $= \dfrac{\text{distance}}{\text{speed}}$
$= \dfrac{1.496 \times 10^{11}}{2.998 \times 10^8}$ seconds
$= 498.999\,332\,9$ seconds
$= 8.316\,655\,548$ minutes

Remember that the question says, 'Give your answer to the nearest minute' … don't lose those well-earned marks by not rounding your answer.
To convert seconds to minutes, you simply divide by 60.

Answer	**How to solve these questions**

Q1 $\frac{5}{9} = 55.555555...\%$

$0.7 = 70\%$

$63\% = 63\%$

Least $= \frac{5}{9}$

Greatest $= 0.7$

In questions of this type, it is best to convert fractions and decimals to percentages.

To convert a fraction to a percentage you just multiply it by 100.

To convert a decimal to a percentage you just multiply it by 100.

Q2 Deposit $= 5\%$ of £740

$\qquad = £37$

Payments $= 12 \times £65$

$\qquad = £780$

Total $= £37 + £780$

$\qquad = £817$

Difference $= £817 - £740$

$\qquad = £77$

For the deposit, find 10% of the cash price (= £74) then halve it to find 5%.

Calculate the total cost of twelve monthly payments of £65 (£780).

Add this to the deposit, to find the total credit price.

Q3 Percentage $= \dfrac{3\,000\,000}{13\,000\,000} \times 100$

$\qquad = 23.076\,923\%$

$\qquad = 23\%$ (to the nearest whole number)

You can find the percentage as:

$\dfrac{3\,000\,000}{13\,000\,000} \times 100$

or more simply $\frac{3}{13} \times 100$ (as both numbers are given in millions).

Remember to give your answer to the nearest whole number or you will lose valuable marks.

Q4 (a) $1.14 \times 35\,000 = 39\,900$

(b) $1.14 \times 39\,900 = 45\,486$

Remember that an increase of 14% gives a multiplier of $\frac{114}{100} = 1.14$.

Alternatively, if you prefer not to use the multiplier method, you can work it out the long way.

Q5 Percentage error $= \dfrac{0.005}{25.005} \times 100$

$\qquad = 0.000\,199\,96\%$

You can use:

percentage error $= \dfrac{\text{error}}{\text{original amount}} \times 100$

where the error $= 25.005 - 25 = 0.005$ kg

and the original amount is the actual weight.

The calculator display of $\boxed{1.9996\ -04}$ or $\boxed{1.9996\ ^{-04}}$ needs to be interpreted.

Q6 $88\% = £550$

$1\% = \dfrac{£550}{88}$

$\qquad = £6.25$

$100\% = 100 \times £6.25$

$\qquad = £625$

Remember that £550 represents $100\% - 12\% = 88\%$ of the original price.

Then 88% of the original price $= £550$

and $\quad$ 1% of the original price $= \dfrac{£550}{88} = £6.25$

so $\quad$ 100% of the original price $= 100 \times £6.25 = £625$

You should always make sure that your answer is reasonable – check it by reducing the price of £625 by 12% (equivalent to a multiplier of 0.88).

Answer	How to solve these questions

Q1 **(a)** 6.5

(a) $\sqrt{42} = 6.48070698\ldots$ $\sqrt{44} = 6.633249581\ldots$
so 6.5 ($= \frac{13}{2}$) is in the range, as are 6.49, 6.51, … and 6.495, 6.505, …
There are countless solutions. It is best to choose one of the most obvious.

(b) 2π

(b) Did you see that 2π (approximately 6.28) satisfies the inequality
$6 < y < 7$?
You could also have suggested $\sqrt{37}, \sqrt{38}, \sqrt{39}, \sqrt{40}, \sqrt{41}, \sqrt{42}, \sqrt{43}, \sqrt{44}, \sqrt{45}, \sqrt{46}, \sqrt{47}, \sqrt{48} \ldots$

(c) $\frac{1}{3}$

(c) You could have written $\frac{1}{3}, \frac{1}{6}, \frac{1}{7}, \frac{1}{9}, \frac{1}{11}, \frac{1}{12}, \ldots$ in fact any fraction which produces a recurring decimal (see Chapter 10 *Recurring decimals*).

Q2 **(a)** $\sqrt{98} = 7\sqrt{2}$
(b) $\sqrt{5} + \sqrt{45} = 4\sqrt{5}$
(c) $\sqrt{6} \times \sqrt{12} = 6\sqrt{2}$

(a) $\sqrt{98} = \sqrt{49 \times 2} = \sqrt{49} \times \sqrt{2} = 7 \times \sqrt{2} = 7\sqrt{2}$
(b) $\sqrt{5} + \sqrt{45} = \sqrt{5} + \sqrt{9 \times 5} = \sqrt{5} + \sqrt{9} \times \sqrt{5} = \sqrt{5} + 3 \times \sqrt{5} = 4\sqrt{5}$
(c) $\sqrt{6} \times \sqrt{12} = \sqrt{6 \times 12} = \sqrt{72} = \sqrt{36 \times 2} = \sqrt{36} \times \sqrt{2} = 6 \times \sqrt{2} = 6\sqrt{2}$

Q3 $\frac{\sqrt{10}}{2}$

For an irrational denominator you should make an equivalent fraction by multiplying the numerator and denominator by the same irrational number.

$$\frac{\sqrt{5}}{\sqrt{2}} = \frac{\sqrt{5} \times \sqrt{2}}{\sqrt{2} \times \sqrt{2}} = \frac{\sqrt{10}}{\sqrt{4}} \quad \text{as } \sqrt{a} \times \sqrt{b} = \sqrt{ab}$$

$$= \frac{\sqrt{10}}{2} \quad \text{as } \sqrt{4} = 2$$

(× $\sqrt{2}$ arrows on numerator and denominator)

Q4 $R = (3 - \sqrt{2})^2 + x$
$R = 11 - 6\sqrt{2} + x$
$x = 6\sqrt{2}$

$R = (3 - \sqrt{2})^2 + x.$
You should start by expanding $(3 - \sqrt{2})^2$.
$(3 - \sqrt{2})^2 = 9 - 3\sqrt{2} - 3\sqrt{2} + 2$ (Remember FOIL).
$R = (3 - \sqrt{2})^2 + x = 9 - 3\sqrt{2} - 3\sqrt{2} + 2 + x = 11 - 6\sqrt{2} + x$
For R to be rational you don't want any surds.
One solution is when x is equal to $6\sqrt{2}$ as $11 - 6\sqrt{2} + 6\sqrt{2} = 11$ (which is rational).

Q5 **(a)** $(3 - \sqrt{5})(4 + \sqrt{5})$
$= 12 + 3\sqrt{5} - 4\sqrt{5} - 5$
$= 7 - \sqrt{5}$
so $a = 7$

(a) $(3 - \sqrt{5})(4 + \sqrt{5}) = a - \sqrt{5}$
Start by expanding (multiplying out the brackets).
$(3 - \sqrt{5})(4 + \sqrt{5}) = 12 - 4\sqrt{5} + 3\sqrt{5} - 5 = 7 - \sqrt{5}$
Now compare the expressions on the right-hand side of the two equations.
$7 - \sqrt{5} = a - \sqrt{5}$ so $a = 7$.

(b) $(3 - \sqrt{5}) \times (4 + \sqrt{5}) + b$
$= 7 - \sqrt{5} + b$
so $b = \sqrt{5}$

(b) $(3 - \sqrt{5})(4 + \sqrt{5}) = 7 - \sqrt{5}$ (as before) so $(3 - \sqrt{5}) \times (4 + \sqrt{5}) + b = 7 - \sqrt{5} + b$
For this to be rational, you don't want any surds.
One possible solution is when b is equal to $\sqrt{5}$ as
$7 - \sqrt{5} + \sqrt{5} = 7$ (which is rational).

Q6 **(a)** $pq - 1 = \sqrt{5} \times \sqrt{10} - 1$
$= \sqrt{50} - 1$
$= 5\sqrt{2} - 1$ (irrational)

(a) Substitute the values you are given into the expression.
The solution $\sqrt{50} - 1$ includes a surd, so it is irrational.

(b) $\frac{q}{pr} = \frac{\sqrt{10}}{\sqrt{5} \times \sqrt{8}} = \frac{\sqrt{10}}{\sqrt{40}}$
$= \sqrt{\frac{10}{40}} = \sqrt{\frac{1}{4}} = \frac{1}{2}$ (rational)

(b) Again, substitute the values you are given into the expression.
In the solution, all the surds cancel out, leaving a rational answer.

(c) $(p + q)^2 = (\sqrt{5} + \sqrt{10})^2$
$= 5 + \sqrt{50} + \sqrt{50} + 10$
$= 15 + 2\sqrt{50}$
$= 15 + 10\sqrt{2}$
(irrational)

(c) Substitute the values you are given into the expression and multiply out the brackets.
This leads to a solution which includes a surd, so the answer is irrational.

Answer	How to solve these questions

Q1 (a) $0.\dot{4} = \frac{4}{9}$

Use the method described in the chapter, to answer this question.
What do you think $0.\dot{9}$ would be?

(b) $0.\dot{5} = \frac{5}{9}$

$0.\dot{7} = \frac{7}{9}$

$0.\dot{8} = \frac{8}{9}$

Q2 $0.\dot{2}\dot{1} = \frac{21}{99} = \frac{7}{33}$

$100 \times \text{(fraction)} = 21.2121212121\ldots$

and $1 \times \text{(fraction)} = 0.2121212121\ldots$

so $99 \times \text{(fraction)} = 21$ (subtracting)

and $\text{(fraction)} = \frac{21}{99}$ (dividing both sides by 99)

You must remember to cancel down or you will lose valuable marks.

Note: It is always a good idea to show all your working, just in case you make an error, so that the examiner can give you marks for the right method.

Q3 $0.\dot{2}4\dot{3} = \frac{243}{999}$

This is a rational number, since it is in the form $\frac{p}{q}$ where p and q are integers.

$1000 \times \text{(fraction)} = 243.243\,243\,243\,243\ldots$

and $1 \times \text{(fraction)} = 0.243\,243\,243\,243\ldots$

so $999 \times \text{(fraction)} = 243$ (subtracting)

and $\text{(fraction)} = \frac{243}{999}$ (dividing both sides by 999)

As $0.\dot{2}4\dot{3} = \frac{243}{999} (= \frac{9}{37})$, it can be written in the form $\frac{p}{q}$ where p and q are integers.
So $0.\dot{2}4\dot{3}$ must be a rational number.

It is always a good idea to give a full description to explain your reasoning.

Q4 $0.\dot{3}\dot{2} = \frac{32}{99}$

so $201.\dot{3}\dot{2} = 201\frac{32}{99}$

Remember that a mixed number consists of a whole number plus a fraction.
Split up $201.\dot{3}\dot{2}$ into a whole number and a decimal fraction.
$201.\dot{3}\dot{2} = 201 + 0.\dot{3}\dot{2}$

Now change the decimal fraction into an ordinary fraction.

$100 \times \text{(fraction)} = 32.323232323232\ldots$

and $1 \times \text{(fraction)} = 0.323232323232\ldots$

so $99 \times \text{(fraction)} = 32$ (subtracting)

and $\text{(fraction)} = \frac{32}{99}$ (dividing both sides by 99)

so $0.\dot{3}\dot{2} = \frac{32}{99}$

Then $201.\dot{3}\dot{2} = 201 + \frac{32}{99} = 201\frac{32}{99}$

Q5 $\frac{1}{9} = 0.11111111\ldots$

$0.7\dot{1} = 0.7 + 0.011111\,11\ldots$

$= 0.7 + 0.11111111 \times \frac{1}{10}$

$= \frac{7}{10} + \frac{1}{9} \times \frac{1}{10}$

$= \frac{7}{10} + \frac{1}{90}$

$= \frac{63}{90} + \frac{1}{90}$

$= \frac{64}{90}$

$= \frac{32}{45}$

First, write down what you know.
$\frac{1}{9} = 0.11111111\ldots$

Now you need to use this fact in your answer.

Split $0.7\dot{1}$ into decimal fractions that you can convert.

$0.7\dot{1} = 0.7 + 0.01111111\ldots$

$0.01111111\ldots = 0.11111111\ldots \div 10$

Remember to cancel down and don't forget how to add and multiply fractions (you may need to revise this again).

| **Answer** | | **How to solve these questions** |

Q1

		Lower	Upper
	(a)	4500	5500
	(b)	4950	5050
	(c)	3.615	3.625
	(d)	235	245
	(e)	$7\frac{1}{4}$	$7\frac{3}{4}$

Remember the rule and apply it, each time.

Q2

Shortest = 6694.5 km

Remember, the bounds are length $\pm \frac{1}{2}$ km (or ± 0.5 km).

Q3

Minimum volume
$= 11.5 \times 8.5 \times 9.5$
$= 928.625 \text{ cm}^3$

Maximum volume
$= 12.5 \times 9.5 \times 10.5$
$= 1246.875 \text{ cm}^3$

For a length of 12 cm the actual values could range from 11.5 cm to 12.5 cm. Similarly, for a length of 9 cm the actual values could range from 8.5 cm to 9.5 cm and for a length of 10 cm the actual values could range from 9.5 cm to 10.5 cm.

The lower bound of the volume is found by multiplying all the minimum values.

$$\text{The lower bound (minimum volume)} = 11.5 \times 8.5 \times 9.5$$
$$= 928.625 \text{ cm}^3$$

$$\text{The upper bound (maximum volume)} = 12.5 \times 9.5 \times 10.5$$
$$= 1246.875 \text{ cm}^3$$

It is always best to use the same vocabulary as is used in the question so use 'lower and upper bounds' here.

Q4

Greatest difference = 8550 − 6250
$= 2300$

For 8500, the minimum is 8450 and the maximum is 8550.

For 6300, the minimum is 6250 and the maximum is 6350.

Remember that the greatest difference will always be between the maximum of the larger value and the minimum of the smaller number. Think about it.

It is useful to work out the minimum and maximum values.

Q5

Smallest possible area of land
$= 28.5\% \times A_{\min}$
$= \frac{28.5}{100} \times 4 \times \pi \times \left(\frac{12\,725}{2}\right)^2$
$= 144\,980\,740.9$
$= 1.449\,807\,409 \times 10^8$
$= 1.45 \times 10^8 \text{ km}^2$ (3 d.p.)

First, remember that the surface area of a sphere is given by $A = 4\pi r^2$ where r is the radius.

Notice also that this question involves the diameter (not the radius) so take care not to make mistakes.

$\text{percentage}_{\min} = 28.5\%$ $\text{percentage}_{\max} = 29.5\%$

$\text{diameter}_{\min} = 12\,725$ km $\text{diameter}_{\max} = 12\,775$ km

$\text{radius} = \dfrac{\text{diameter}}{2}$ so $\text{radius}_{\min} = \dfrac{12\,725}{2} = 6362.5$ km

Remember to round your answer to an appropriate degree of accuracy.

Q6 Maximum speed = $\dfrac{65.5}{0.575}$

= 113.913 043 5

= 114 kph (3 s.f.)

Minimum speed = $\dfrac{64.5}{0.591\,666\,666}$

= 109 kph (3 s.f.)

First, find the minimum and maximum values:

distance$_{min}$ = 64.5 km   distance$_{max}$ = 65.5 km

time$_{min}$ = 34.5 minutes   time$_{max}$ = 35.5 minutes

Then use:

$$speed = \dfrac{distance}{time}$$

and remember that time must be expressed in hours.

34.5 minutes = $\dfrac{34.5}{60}$ = 0.575 hours

35.5 minutes = $\dfrac{35.5}{60}$ = 0.591 666 666 hours

So speed$_{max}$ = $\dfrac{65.5}{0.575}$ = 113.913 043 5 kph

And speed$_{min}$ = $\dfrac{64.5}{0.591\,666\,666}$ = 109.014 084 5 kph

Finally, round your answer to a reasonable degree of accuracy (say 3 s.f. here).

Chapter 12 Cumulative frequency

Q1 Range = 28 cm

Interquartile range = 23 cm

Start by arranging the information in order.

10, 12, 13, 13, 16, 18, 18, 19, 20, 20, 21, 36, 37, 37, 38

The range of the heights is 38 − 10 = 28 cm.

To find the interquartile range you need to find the lower quartile and the upper quartile. The lower quartile is the $\frac{1}{4}(15 + 1)$ = 4th value and the upper quartile is the $\frac{3}{4}(15 + 1)$ = 12th value.

From the data (all measured in cm):

10, 12, 13, 13, 16, 18, 18, 19, 20, 20, 21, 36, 37, 37, 38

Lower quartile   Median   Upper quartile

Interquartile range = upper quartile − lower quartile = 36 − 13

= 23 cm

Q2

Start by completing the cumulative frequency table.

Lifetime (hours)	Frequency	Cumulative frequency
100–199	32	32
200–299	98	130
300–399	65	195
400–499	14	209
500–599	3	212
600–699	2	214

Then draw the curve, as shown.

Note: The upper values of the class intervals are $199\frac{1}{2}$, $299\frac{1}{2}$, $399\frac{1}{2}$ as the lifetime is given to the nearest hour.

From the graph:

(a) 60 batteries lasted less than 250 hours.

(b) 39 batteries lasted more than 350 hours.

(a) 60 batteries lasted less than 250 hours

(b) 175 batteries lasted less than 350 hours
so 214 − 175 = 39 lasted more than 350 hours.

(c) Median = 282
Interquartile range = 100

(c) median = 282 (read off value)
upper quartile = 320 (read off value)
lower quartile = 220 (read off value)

interquartile range = upper quartile − lower quartile
= 320 − 220
= 100

Q3 (a)

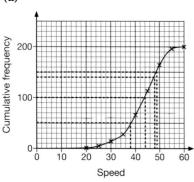

(a) Draw the curve from the table.

Note: The upper values of the class intervals are clearly 20, 25, 30, 35 … here.

(b) **(i)** Median = 44 mph

(ii) Interquartile range
= 11 mph

(iii) Percentage of cars
travelling at less than
48 mph = 70%

(b) **(i)** Median = 44 mph

(ii) LQ = 38
UQ = 49

Interquartile range = 49 − 38
= 11 mph

(iii) Number of cars travelling at less than 48 mph = 140

Percentage of cars = $\frac{140}{200} \times 100\%$
= 70%

Q4 (a) See the table opposite.

(a)

Time	$t < 10$	$t < 15$	$t < 20$	$t < 25$
Frequency	0	2	6	13

Time	$t < 30$	$t < 35$	$t < 40$	$t < 45$
Frequency	28	42	47	48

(b)

(b) Use the table to draw the curve.

(c) Median arrival time = 7.29 a.m.

(c) Calculate the median arrival time using a cumulative frequency value of 24. Median time of arrival = 7.29 a.m.

(d) **(i)** Time of arrival = 7.24 a.m.

(ii) Petra waited 8 minutes.

(d) **(i)** Find the time of arrival, by scanning across from the cumulative frequency of 12. Read the corresponding time (24 minutes), and add on to 7 a.m. Petra's time of arrival = 7.24 a.m.

(ii) Use a cumulative frequency value of $\frac{3}{4} \times 48 = 36$ to find when the coach arrived. This gives a time of 32 minutes, so the coach arrived at 7.32 a.m. Petra arrived at 7.24 a.m, so she waited 8 minutes.

(e) 12 people arrived after Karen.

(e) Now find the cumulative frequency at time = 32 minutes and subtract from 48, to find the number of people that arrived after Karen. **Number of people who arrived after Karen = 12.**

Q5 **(a)** Median height of the boys
= 168 cm

(a)

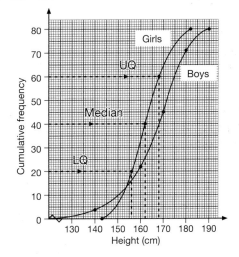

Median height is at 40th value. Median = 168 cm.

(b) Interquartile range = 17 cm

(b) Draw lines at the 20th and 60th values to calculate the interquartile range.
IQR = 175 − 158 = 17 cm

(c) **(i)** See the diagram opposite.

(c) **(i)**

(ii) Boys have a bigger median
height. Boys' heights are
more spread out.

Chapter 13 Mode, median and mean

Q1 **(a)**

Time (t) seconds	Tally	Frequency
$0 \leqslant t < 5$	///	3
$5 \leqslant t < 10$	⧸⧸⧸⧸⧸ //	7
$10 \leqslant t < 15$	⧸⧸⧸⧸⧸ ////	9
$15 \leqslant t < 20$	////	4
$20 \leqslant t < 25$	//	2

(a) The tallies are a useful way of recording the items of data. When you have finished, make sure that the total is the same as the number of entries in the table you started with.

Be careful to include 10.0 in the $10 \leqslant t < 15$ group.

(b) 10–15

(b) The modal class interval is the one with the largest frequency, which is $10 \leqslant t < 15$.

Q2 **(a)** **(i)** Median runs per ball is 2.

(ii) Mean is 2.28.

(a) **(i)** You need to look at the 13th value. The median number of runs per ball is 2.

(ii)

Runs	Frequency	Frequency × runs
x	f	fx
0	3	0
1	8	8
2	4	8
3	3	9
4	5	20
5	0	0
6	2	12
	$\sum f = 25$	$\sum fx = 57$

$$\text{Mean} = \frac{\sum fx}{\sum f} = \frac{57}{25} = 2.28$$

(b) **(i)** New median is 3.

(b) **(i)** Add the new totals and amend the table.

Runs	Frequency	Frequency × runs
x	f	fx
0	3	0
1	8	8
2	4	8
3	4	12
4	7	28
5	1	5
6	3	18
	$\sum f = 30$	$\sum fx = 79$

Now you need to look at the $15\frac{1}{2}$th value.
The median of runs per ball is 3.

(ii) New mean = 2.63 (3 s.f.).

(ii) $\sum f = 25 + 5 = 30$
$\sum fx = 57 + 4 + 4 + 5 + 3 + 6 = 79$
$$\text{Mean} = \frac{\sum fx}{\sum f} = \frac{79}{30} = 2.633\,333\,333$$
$$= 2.63 \text{ (3 s.f.)}$$

(c) The mean takes account of all the values.

(c) The mean takes account of all values and gives due weighting to the high number of 1s and 4s.

Q3 **(a)** **(i)** Range = 12 cm

(a) **(i)** Remember that the range should always be given as a single figure. The range of the lengths = 39 − 27 = 12 cm.

(ii) Mean length = 32 cm

(ii) Mean length
$$= \frac{27 + 28 + 29 + 30 + 31 + 31 + 32 + 33 + 35 + 37 + 39}{11}$$
$$= \frac{352}{11}$$
$$= 32 \text{ cm}$$

(b) The Spanish cucumbers have a smaller average length and their lengths are less spread out.

(b) The range is smaller for the Spanish cucumbers, so the lengths are not so spread out.

The Spanish cucumbers also have a smaller average length.

How to solve these questions

 Q4 **(a)** Range = 5 g

(b) Mean weight = 457 g (3 s.f.)

(a) The range of the weights in the table = 460 – 455 = 5 g

(b)

Weight (g)	Number of jars	
x	f	fx
454	0	0
455	1	455
456	6	2736
457	7	3199
458	3	1374
459	1	459
460	2	920
	$\sum f = 20$	$\sum fx = 9143$

For the frequency distribution, the mean $= \dfrac{\sum fx}{\sum f}$

$$= \frac{9143}{20}$$

$$= 457.15$$

$$= 457 \text{ g (3 s.f.)}$$

Q5 Mean = 17 minutes
(to the nearest minute)

Time, t (mins)	Number of people	Mid-interval value	Frequency × mid-interval value
$0 < t \leqslant 10$	4	5	20
$10 < t \leqslant 20$	7	15	105
$20 < t \leqslant 30$	3	25	75
$30 < t \leqslant 40$	2	35	70
	$\sum f = 16$		$\sum fx = 270$

$$\text{Mean} = \frac{\sum fx}{\sum f}$$

$$= \frac{270}{16}$$

$$= 16.875$$

$$= 17 \text{ minutes (to the nearest minute)}$$

Q6 Mean height = 43 cm (2 s.f.)

Height	Frequency	Mid-interval value	Frequency × mid interval value
	f	x	$f \times x$
15–20	8	17.5	$8 \times 17.5 = 140$
20–30	4	25	$4 \times 25 = 100$
30–40	5	35	$5 \times 35 = 175$
40–50	11	45	$11 \times 45 = 495$
50–60	17	55	$17 \times 55 = 935$
60–70	2	65	$2 \times 65 = 130$
70–80	1	75	$1 \times 75 = 75$
	$\sum f = 48$		$\sum fx = 2050$

For the group frequency distribution, mean $= \dfrac{\sum fx}{\sum f} = \dfrac{2050}{48}$

$$= 42.708\,333\,33$$

$$= 43 \text{ cm to an appropriate degree of accuracy}$$

Answer

How to solve these questions

Q7 **(a)** Mean height = 162 cm (3 s.f.)

(a)

Height, h (cm)	Frequency	Mid-interval values	Frequency × mid interval values
$140 \leqslant h < 148$	6	144	864
$148 \leqslant h < 156$	10	152	1520
$156 \leqslant h < 164$	15	160	2400
$164 \leqslant h < 172$	18	168	3024
$172 \leqslant h < 180$	11	176	1936
	$\sum f = 60$		$\sum fx = 9744$

An estimate of the mean $= \dfrac{\sum fx}{\sum f}$

$= \dfrac{9744}{60}$

$= 162.4$

$= 162$ cm (3 s.f.)

(b) The median is the 30th value, and this value will be in the 156–164 cm group.

(b) The median is the middle value (i.e. the 30th value) which lies in the $156 \leqslant h \leqslant 164$ group so that the median lies between 156 cm and 164 cm.

(c)

(c) Use the table to draw the histogram.

Since the class intervals are all equal, the histogram is similar to a barchart.

Chapter 14 Scatter diagrams

Answer

How to solve these questions

Q1

The relationship is strong and positive. The point $(7\frac{1}{2}, 100)$ is likely to be an error.

Use the table to plot the information on a graph.

Look at the shape of the graph and the pattern formed by the dots to make a comment on the correlation.

Q2 **(a)**

(a) Plot the points and add the line of best fit, to pass through as many points as you can, but make sure that there are equal numbers of points on either side of the line.

(b) **(i)** The distance thrown
= 6.1 m
(ii) The arm length = 46 cm

(b) You can add lines to your graph, if it helps to find the answers.
(i) The distance thrown for an arm length of 50 cm = 6.1 m
(ii) The arm length for a distance of 5.5 m thrown = 46 cm

Q3 **(a)** See the diagram opposite.

Look carefully at the points and try to draw the line of best fit through as many as possible, with equal numbers on either side.

(b) **(i)** Height after 10 days
= 11 cm
(ii) Height after 20 days
= 23 cm

(b) Use the line of best fit to find:
(i) height after 10 days = 11 cm
(ii) height after 20 days = 23 cm

(c) Answer (i) is more likely to be reliable because it is nearer the middle of the range, rather than close to one end.

(c) The answer which is more likely to be more reliable is **(i)**.
This is because it is in the middle of the range. 20 days is beyond one of the limits.

Q4 **(a)** See the diagram opposite.

(a) Use the figures to draw the scatter diagram.

(b) There seems to be strong positive correlation between adult literacy and life expectancy.

(b) Look carefully at the graph and see if there is a pattern. Describe any correlation that you can see between the 'Adult literacy' and the 'Life expectancy' figures.

(c) Life expectancy of an adult from a country with 42% adult literacy = 52 years.

(c) Draw a line of best fit. From the graph, the life expectancy of an adult from a country with 42% adult literacy = 52 years.

(d) Yes, it does seem reasonable since there seems to be positive correlation between the two sets of figures. It would also be reasonable to think that where adult literacy is high, the population would be able to read about healthy living.

(d) Think of a reason for your answer.

Chapter 15 Probability

Q1 **(a)** **(i)** Might be correct
(ii) Must be correct
(iii) Must be wrong

(a) **(i)** The probability that the marble is red is $\frac{1}{2}$ might be correct.
(ii) The probability that the marble is red or blue is 1 must be correct.
(iii) The probability that the marble is red is -0.4 must be wrong.

(b) **(i)** $\frac{1}{3}$
(ii) $\frac{7}{12}$
(iii) 0

(b) **(i)** p(blue) $= \frac{4}{12} = \frac{1}{3}$ (cancel wherever possible)
(ii) p(blue or red) $= \frac{7}{12}$
(iii) p(yellow) $= 0$ (impossible)

Q2 **(a)** $\frac{3}{10}$

(a) p(a blue Ford is chosen from the cars)$= \dfrac{\text{number of blue Fords}}{\text{number of cars}} = \frac{6}{20} = \frac{3}{10}$

(b) $\frac{7}{10}$

(b) p(a Vauxhall is chosen from the white cars) $= \dfrac{\text{number of Vauxhalls}}{\text{number of white cars}} = \frac{7}{10}$

Q3 **(a)** $\frac{2}{5}$

(a) p(two occupants) $= \frac{20}{50} = \frac{2}{5}$

(b) 120

(b) Total number of car occupants $= 13 \times 1 + 20 \times 2 + 3 \times 3 + 12 \times 4 + 2 \times 5$
$$= 13 + 40 + 9 + 48 + 10$$
$$= 120$$

(c) **(i)** $\frac{5}{12}$

(c) **(i)** p(driving a car) $= \frac{50}{120} = \frac{5}{12}$ (as there were 50 cars therefore 50 drivers)

(ii) $\frac{1}{4}$

(ii) p(a passenger from a car with four occupants) $= \frac{1}{4}$
(a car with 4 occupants has 1 driver and 4 occupants so probability $= \frac{1}{4}$)

| **Answer** | **How to solve these questions** |

Q4 **(a)** $\frac{3}{5}$

(b) See the diagram opposite.

(a) Relative frequency $= \frac{12}{20} = \frac{3}{5}$

(b) Use the data to draw the graph to show the relative frequency of throwing a head.

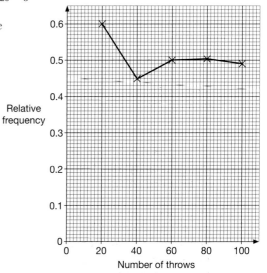

Number of throws	20	40	60	80	100
Number of heads	12	18	30	42	49
Relative frequency	$\frac{12}{20} = 0.6$	$\frac{18}{40} = 0.45$	$\frac{30}{60} = 0.5$	$\frac{42}{80} = 0.525$	$\frac{49}{100} = 0.49$

The relative frequency is tending towards 0.5.

(c) 500

(c) Relative frequency of throwing a head for 1000 throws
$= 1000 \times \frac{1}{2} = 500$

Q5 **(a)**

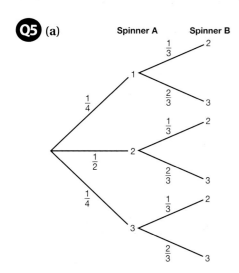

(a) Use the information you are given to complete the diagram.

(b) $p(3,3) = \frac{1}{6}$

(b) p(getting a score of 3 with each spinner) $= \frac{1}{4} \times \frac{4}{6} = \frac{1}{6}$

Draw a space diagram to show 24 possibilities and their totals.

(c) p(a total score of 5) $= \frac{10}{24}$

(c) p(a total score of 5) $= \frac{10}{24}$
(see circled answers above)

Q6

Draw a space diagram to show the totals.

Totals

	5	6	7	8	9	10
	4	5	6	7	8	9
Spinner	3	4	5	6	7	8
2	2	3	4	5	6	7
	1	2	3	4	5	6
		1	2	3	4	5

Spinner 1

(a) p(total is 10) = $\frac{1}{25}$

(b) p(total is 9) = $\frac{2}{25}$

(c) $\frac{3}{25}$

(d) $\frac{1}{125}$

(a) p(total is 10) = $\frac{1}{25}$

(b) p(total is 9) = $\frac{2}{25}$

(c) p(total is 3 or less) = p(total is 2 or total is 3)
$$= \text{p(total is 2)} + \text{p(total is 3)}$$
$$= \frac{1}{25} + \frac{2}{25} = \frac{3}{25}$$

(d) p(all three spinners show 5) = $\frac{1}{5} \times \frac{1}{5} \times \frac{1}{5} = \frac{1}{125}$

Q7 (a) (1, Heads), (1, Tails),
(2, Heads), (2, Tails),
(3, Heads), (3, Tails),
(4, Heads), (4, Tails),
(5, Heads), (5, Tails)

(b) **(i)** 0.14

(ii) 0
(iii) The spinner is most likely to land on 1.
(iv) 0.25

(c) 0.125

(a) Make sure that you list all of the possible outcomes. Be systematic, don't just write them down in any order.

(b) **(i)** p(spinner lands on 5) = 1 − (0.36 + 0.1 + 0.25 + 0.15)
$$= 1 − 0.86 = 0.14$$

(ii) p(spinner lands on 6) = 0 (no chance of it landing on 6)
(iii) The spinner is most likely to land on 1. (This value has the highest probability so must be most likely.)
(iv) p(spinner lands on an even number) = p(2 or 4) = 0.1 + 0.15 = 0.25

(c) p(spinner lands on 3 and the coins shows Heads) = 0.25 × $\frac{1}{2}$ = 0.125

Chapter 16 Histograms

Q1

Add a column to the table for the frequency density, and complete it.
(Remember, frequency density = frequency ÷ class width, so calculate 16 ÷ 0.5, 28 ÷ 0.5, 26 ÷ 1, 12 ÷ 1, 18 ÷ 2.)

Time t (hours)	Frequency	Class width	Frequency density
$0 \leqslant t < 0.5$	16	0.5	$\frac{16}{0.5} = 32$
$0.5 \leqslant t < 1$	28	0.5	$\frac{28}{0.5} = 56$
$1 \leqslant t < 2$	26	1	$\frac{26}{1} = 26$
$2 \leqslant t < 3$	12	1	$\frac{12}{1} = 12$
$3 \leqslant t < 5$	18	2	$\frac{18}{2} = 9$

Use these frequency densities to draw the histogram.

Q2 **(a)**

(b) 65 cars were probably speeding.

Q3 **(a)** See the diagram opposite.

Q4 **(a)** £453 (to the nearest £)

(a) Add the frequency densities of $6 \div 15$, $19 \div 10$, $34 \div 10$, $26 \div 10$, $15 \div 20$ to the chart. Use the chart to draw a histogram.

Speed (s km/h)	$20 \leqslant s < 35$	$35 \leqslant s < 45$	$45 \leqslant s < 55$	$55 \leqslant s < 65$	$65 \leqslant s < 85$
Frequency	6	19	34	26	15
Class width	15	10	10	10	20
Frequency density	$\frac{6}{15} = 0.4$	$\frac{19}{10} = 1.9$	$\frac{34}{10} = 3.4$	$\frac{26}{10} = 2.6$	$\frac{15}{20} = 0.75$

(b) Draw a line at speed = 48 km/h.

Estimate the area to the right of line and convert it back to give
$3.4 \times 7 + 2.6 \times 10 + 0.75 \times 20 = 65.8$

So 65 cars cars were probably speeding.

Draw a table and calculate the respective frequency densities.

Height (cm)	Frequency	Class width	Frequency density
15–19	4	5	$\frac{4}{5} = 0.8$
20–24	6	5	$\frac{6}{5} = 1.2$
25–29	7	5	$\frac{7}{5} = 1.4$
30–39	11	10	$\frac{11}{10} = 1.1$
40–49	9	10	$\frac{9}{10} = 0.9$
50–74	5	25	$\frac{5}{25} = 0.2$
75–99	2	25	$\frac{2}{25} = 0.08$

Remember that the heights are given to the nearest cm so the 15–19 group includes plants from $14\frac{1}{2}$ cm to $19\frac{1}{2}$, so class width = 5, etc.

(a) To estimate the mean, draw a table with a column to show mid-interval values (100, 300, 500, 800, 1500) and a column for frequency × price (6×100, 21×300, 17×500, 7×800, 2×1500).

Price (£p)	Mid-interval value	Frequency	MIV × frequency
$0 \leqslant p < 200$	100	6	600
$200 \leqslant p < 400$	300	21	6300
$400 \leqslant p < 600$	500	17	8500
$600 \leqslant p < 1000$	800	7	5600
$1000 \leqslant p < 2000$	1500	2	3000
		$\sum f = 53$	$\sum fx = 24\,000$

Mean $= \dfrac{24\,000}{53} = £452.830\,188\,7 = £453$ (to the nearest pound)

(b) See the diagram opposite.

(b) Add columns for the class width and frequency density, like this.

Price (£p)	Mid-interval value	Frequency	MIV × frequency	Class width	Frequency density
$0 \leqslant p < 200$	100	6	600	200	$\frac{6}{200} = 0.03$
$200 \leqslant p < 400$	300	21	6300	200	$\frac{21}{200} = 0.105$
$400 \leqslant p < 600$	500	17	8500	200	$\frac{17}{200} = 0.085$
$600 \leqslant p < 1000$	800	7	5600	400	$\frac{7}{400} = 0.0175$
$1000 \leqslant p < 2000$	1500	2	3000	1000	$\frac{2}{1000} = 0.002$
		$\sum f = 53$	$\sum fx = 24\,000$		

Draw the histogram, using the information in the table.

(c) 213

(c) The number of cameras available in May 1997

$= 200 \times 0.005 + 200 \times 0.15 + 200 \times 0.35 + 400 \times 0.275 + 1000 \times 0.002$

$= 213$

(d) The mean price of cameras in May 1997 was greater than the mean price of cameras in December 1997.

There was a greater proportion of cameras in the £600–1000 price range in May 1997 than in December 1997.

(d) You are asked to compare, in two ways, the prices of cameras in December 1997 with the prices in May 1997, so you need to look carefully at the information and the graphs and draw two different conclusions from the data presented.

Q5 **(a)**

Lifetime, x (1000s hours)	Number of bulbs, f	Frequency density
$6 \leqslant x < 10$	4	1
$10 \leqslant x < 12$	15	7.5
$12 \leqslant x < 14$	19	8.5
$14 \leqslant x < 16$	8	4
$16 \leqslant x < 20$	4	1

(a) Complete the frequency density column in the table ($4 \div 4$, $15 \div 2$, $19 \div 2$, $8 \div 2$, $4 \div 4$) and draw the histogram.

Lifetime, x (1000s hours)	Number of bulbs, f	Class width	Frequency density
$6 \leqslant x < 10$	4	4	$\frac{4}{4} = 1$
$10 \leqslant x < 12$	15	2	$\frac{15}{2} = 7.5$
$12 \leqslant x < 14$	19	2	$\frac{19}{2} = 8.5$
$14 \leqslant x < 16$	8	2	$\frac{8}{2} = 4$
$16 \leqslant x < 20$	4	4	$\frac{4}{4} = 1$

See the diagram opposite.

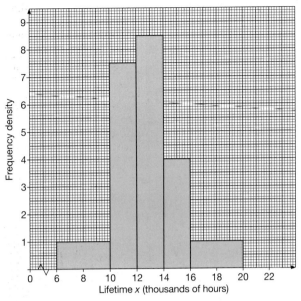

(b) 48%

(b) To find the total number of bulbs, you need to find the total area under the histogram.

$$2 \times 3 + 2 \times 6 + 2 \times 8 + 2 \times 5 + 4 \times 1.5 = 50$$

The number that last longer than 15 000 hours is:

$$1 \times 8 + 2 \times 5 + 4 \times 1.5 = 24$$

Proportion $= \frac{24}{50} = 48\%$

(c) The second company's bulbs are more environmentally-friendly.

(c) For the first company, the proportion of bulbs that last longer than 15 000 hours $= \frac{8}{50} = 16\%$.

So the second company manufactures the more environmentally-friendly light bulbs, as the proportion of bulbs that last longer than 15 000 hours is higher.

Chapter 17 Further probability

Answer

How to solve these questions

Q1 (a)

first ball   second ball

red $\frac{4}{10}$
 → red $\frac{3}{9}$
 → blue $\frac{6}{9}$

blue $\frac{6}{10}$
 → red $\frac{4}{9}$
 → blue $\frac{5}{9}$

p(red and red) $= \frac{2}{15}$

(b) p(red and blue or blue and red) $= \frac{8}{15}$

(a) From the diagram:

probability of obtaining two red balls = p(red and red)

$$= \frac{4}{10} \times \frac{3}{9}$$
$$= \frac{12}{90}$$
$$= \frac{2}{15}$$

(b) From the diagram:

probability of obtaining one ball of each colour

$$= \text{p(red and blue or blue and red)}$$
$$= \frac{4}{10} \times \frac{6}{9} + \frac{6}{10} \times \frac{4}{9}$$
$$= \frac{24}{90} + \frac{24}{90}$$
$$= \frac{48}{90}$$
$$= \frac{8}{15}$$

Q2 **(a)** p(red and red and red) = $\frac{1}{22}$

(a) p(three discs drawn are red) = p (red and red and red)

$$= \frac{5}{12} \times \frac{4}{11} \times \frac{3}{10}$$

$$= \frac{1}{22}$$

(b) p(RRR) + p(BBB) = $\frac{7}{110}$

(b) p(three discs drawn are of the same colour) = p(RRR) + p(BBB)

$$= \frac{1}{22} + (\frac{4}{12} \times \frac{3}{11} \times \frac{2}{10})$$

$$= \frac{1}{22} + \frac{1}{55} = \frac{7}{110}$$

(c) p(RRX + RXR + XRR) = $\frac{7}{22}$

(c) exactly two of the discs drawn are red = p(RRX + RXR + XRR)

$$= 3 \times (\frac{5}{12} \times \frac{4}{11} \times \frac{7}{10})$$

$$= \frac{7}{22}$$

Q3 **(a)** p(Q or R) = 0.55

(a) p(Q or R) = p(Q) + p(R)

$$= 30\% + \frac{1}{4}$$

$$= 0.30 + 0.25$$

$$= 0.55$$

(b) p(R or S) = 0.45

(b) p(R or S) = p(R) + p(S)

$$= \frac{1}{4} + 0.2$$

$$= 0.25 + 0.2$$

$$= 0.45$$

(c) p(Q or R or S) = 0.75

(c) p(Q or R or S) = p(Q) + p(R) + p(S)

$$= 30\% + \frac{1}{4} + 0.2$$

$$= 0.30 + 0.25 + 0.2$$

$$= 0.75$$

You can give your answers in fractions, decimals or percentages.

Q4

This question looks tricky, but you can use algebra to help you!

Let p be the probability of a score of 1.

p(1) = p
p(2) = p
p(3) = p
p(4) = p
p(5) = $2p$ (a score of 5 is twice as likely as a score of 4)
p(6) = $4p$ (a score of 6 is twice as likely as a score of 5)

So $p + p + p + p + 2p + 4p = 1$
$10p = 1$ (total of probabilities of all outcomes = 1)
so $p = \frac{1}{10}$

Now it is quite straightforward.

(a) p(a score of 6) = $\frac{2}{5}$

(a) p(a score of 6) = $4p = \frac{4}{10} = \frac{2}{5}$

(b) p(a score of 5) = $\frac{1}{5}$

(b) p(a score of 5) = $2p = \frac{2}{10} = \frac{1}{5}$

(c) p(a score less than 4) = $\frac{3}{10}$

(c) p(a score less than 4) = p(1) + p(2) + p(3)

$$= p + p + p$$

$$= 3p$$

$$= \frac{3}{10}$$

Q5 **(a)**

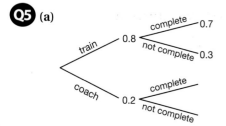

(a) Construct the tree diagram and label it.
Use the fact that 80% = 0.8 and 70% = 0.7.

(b) 0.24

(c)

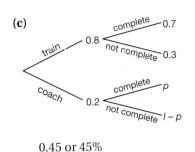

0.45 or 45%

(b) From the diagram:
p(travel by train but does not complete crossword) $= 0.8 \times 0.3$
$= 0.24$

(c) Again, algebra can come to the rescue.

Let p be the probability of Miss Mutch completing her crossword on a day when she travels by coach. (Mark this on the diagram.)

Then
$$0.8 \times 0.7 + 0.2 \times p = 0.65$$
$$0.56 + 0.2p = 0.65$$
$$0.2p = 0.09$$
$$p = \frac{0.09}{0.2}$$
$$p = 0.45 \text{ (or } 45\%)$$

Chapter 18 Patterns and sequences

Answer ◄ **How to solve these questions**

Q1 **(a)** 1, 3, 5, 7, 9, …

(b) 0, 2, 6, 12, 20, …

(c) $\frac{1}{2}, \frac{2}{3}, \frac{3}{4}, \frac{4}{5}, \frac{5}{6}, …$

Substitute values 1, 2, 3, 4, 5 in the expression for the nth term.

Q2 **(a)** 19

(b) **(i)** $x + 4$

(ii) $x - 4$

(a) You find each term by adding 4 to the previous term.

(b) **(i)** The next term will be x add 4 or $x + 4$.

(ii) Remember, you can find the term before x by taking 4 away from x, to give $x - 4$.

Q3 **(a)** nth term $= 3n$

(b) nth term $= 3n - 2$

(c) n^2

(d) $4n^2$ or $(2n)^2$

(a) Note that the numbers are all in the 3× table.

(b) The common difference is +3 and the nth term is $3n - 2$.

(c) You should recognise these as square numbers.

(d) These are also the square numbers but you need to find the rule by looking at the first term.

Q4 **(a)** 95, 191

(b) Each term $= 2 \times$ previous term $+ 1$

(c) $\dfrac{n}{n + 3}$

(a) The sequence is 2, 5, 11, 23, 47, …

The first differences are +3, +6, +12, +24, …

Did you recognise that each term $= 2 \times$ previous term $+ 1$?

(b) You need to explain how you get from one term of the sequence to the next term.

(c) The numbers on the top form one sequence, the numbers on the bottom form another. Did you spot it?

Q5 **(a)** nth term $= 3n - 1$

(b) **(i)** $-\frac{1}{2}, 0$

(ii) $n^2 - 2n - 80 = 0.$
$(n + 8)(n - 10) = 0$
$n = -8$ or $n = 10$
so the value of n is 10.

(a) The common difference is +3 so the nth term is $3n - 1$.

(b) **(i)** Substitute 1 and 2 in the formula $\frac{1}{2}(n^2 - 2n)$.

(ii) Solving the quadratic $n^2 - 2n - 80 = 0$ gives $n = -8$ or $n = 10$. Reject the value $n = -8$ as it is unreasonable.

See Chapter 21, *Quadratic equations* for further information.

Q6 **(a)** 10 squares

(a)

(b) $2n+2$

(b)

The fourth pattern (pattern 4) gives:
$4+4+1+1$

The fifth pattern (pattern 5) gives:
$5+5+1+1$

So the nth pattern gives:

$n+n+1+1$

i.e. $n+n+2$ or $2n+2$ (simplifying)

Q7 The nth pattern has $2n+1$ matches.

1st	2nd	3rd	nth
Pattern 1	Pattern 2	Pattern 3	Pattern n
3 matches	3 matches + 2	3 matches + 2 + 2	3 matches + 2 + 2 + 2 + ... + 2

There will be $(n-1)$ lots of 2, so the nth term $= 3 + (n-1) \times 2$

$$= 3 + 2n - 2$$
$$= 2n + 1$$

Chapter 19 Manipulation of equations

Q1 **(a)**
$$r = 4pq - s$$
$$s + r = 4pq$$
$$s = 4pq - r$$

(b)
$$r = 4pq - s$$
$$r + s = 4pq$$
$$4pq = r + s$$
$$q = \frac{r+s}{4p}$$

Remember that you must do the same thing to both sides, to keep the equation correct and balanced.

Q2 $\dfrac{bc^2}{d} = 6$

$$bc^2 = 6d$$

$$c^2 = \frac{6d}{b}$$

$$c = \sqrt{\frac{6d}{b}}$$

Multiply both sides by d.

Divide both sides by b.

Take the square root of both sides.

Q3 **(a)** $16 \times x + 4 \times (2x + 3)$
$16x + 8x + 12$
$24x + 12$

(a) 16 small slabs weigh $16 \times x$ kg
4 large slabs weigh $4 \times (2x + 3)$ kg.
Remember to give the answer in its simplest form.

(b) $24x + 12 = 132$
$24x + 12 - 12 = 132 - 12$
$24x = 120$
$x = \frac{120}{24}$
$x = 5$

(b) As the total weight of the slabs is 132 kilograms, set it equal to the expression from part (a).

Q4 **(a)** **(i)** $P = 3x + 2 + 2x + 3x + 2 + 2x$
$P = 10x + 4$ cm

(ii) $A = (3x + 2)(2x)$
$A = 2x(3x + 2)$ cm^2

Remember that:
the perimeter of a rectangle = $2l + 2b$ the area of a rectangle = $l \times b$.

perimeter $= l + b + l + b$
$= 2l + 2b$

area $= l \times b$

(b) $10x + 4 = 44$ (as $P = 44$)
$10x = 40$
$x = 4$
$A = 2x(3x + 2)$
Substituting $x = 4$:
$A = 2 \times 4(3 \times 4 + 2)$
$A = 112$ cm^2

Q5 **(i)**

Area $= hb + 2hb + 3hb$
$= 6hb$

(i) Split the shape into three areas, then find the areas of the three parts. Then use what you know to solve the problem.

(ii) $6hb = 3240$
$6 \times h \times 36 = 3240$
$h = 15$ cm

(ii) Use the fact that the area is 3240 cm^2 and b is 36 cm.

Q6 **(a)** £$30x$

(a) Neil spent $30 \times$ £x.

(b) £$10x + 10$

(b) Originally, each share costs £x.
So if the price of each share has risen by £1
the new cost is £$x + 1$.
10 shares cost $10 \times$ £$x + 1$ or £$10x + 10$.

(c) £$40x$

(c) Originally, each share costs £x.
So if the price of each share has doubled:
new cost is $2 \times$ £x or £$2x$.
20 shares cost $20 \times$ £$2x$ or £$40x$.

(d) $50x + 10 - 30x = 70$
$20x + 10 = 70$
$20x = 60$
$x = 3$
Original cost of share = £3

(d) Expenditure in pounds = $30x$
Income in pounds = $10x + 10 + 40x = 50x + 10$.
Difference in pounds = 70
So $50x + 10 - 30x = 70$
Solve this equation to find $x = 3$.

Answer

How to solve these questions

Q1
$$2x + 3y = 7$$
$$5x - 3y = 21$$
$$7x = 28$$
$$x = 4$$

$$2x + 3y = 7$$
$$8 + 3y = 7$$
$$3y = -1$$
$$y = -\tfrac{1}{3}$$

In this example, the y terms are numerically equal and the signs are opposite. You can add the equations to remove y.

This is the elimination method.

Q2
$$5x + 3y = 19$$
$$5x - 2y = 4$$
$$3y - (-2y) = 15$$
$$5y = 15$$
$$y = 3$$

$$5x + 3y = 19$$
$$5x + 9 = 19$$
$$5x = 10$$
$$x = 2$$

In this example, the x terms are numerically equal and the signs are the same (i.e. both positive), so you can subtract one equation from the other to eliminate x.
This is the elimination method.

Q3
$$2x + 3y = 1$$
$$x - 2y = 11$$

Substituting $x = 11 + 2y$:
$$2x + 3y = 1$$
$$2(11 + 2y) + 3y = 1$$
$$22 + 4y + 3y = 1$$
$$7y = -21$$
$$y = -3$$

$$x = 11 + 2y$$
$$x = 11 + 2 \times -3$$
$$x = 11 - 6$$
$$x = 5$$

You will probably find that the method of substitution is best for this question.
Here are some possible substitutions:

$x = \dfrac{1 - 3y}{2}$ (from the first equation)

$y = \dfrac{1 - 2x}{3}$ (from the first equation)

$x = 11 + 2y$ (from the second equation)

$y = \dfrac{x - 11}{2}$ (from the second equation)

There is a single term in x in the second equation, so it will be easier to turn this into an expression for x. Then you can substitute for x in the first equation.

Q4
$$x + y = 13$$
$$x - y = 3$$
$$2x = 16$$
$$x = 8$$
$$x + y = 13$$
$$8 + y = 13$$
$$y = 5$$

Let your two numbers be x and y. Then form two equations.
- If they have a sum of 13 then $x + y = 13$.
- If they have a difference of 3 then $x - y = 3$.
Solve the equations using the method you like best.

Answer	How to solve these questions

Q5
$x + y = 8$

$y = 3x - 4$

Substitute $y = 3x - 4$ in the first equation.

$x + y = 8$

$x + (3x - 4) = 8$

$x + 3x - 4 = 8$

$4x - 4 = 8$

$4x = 12$

$x = 3$

$x + y = 8$

$3 + y = 8$

$y = 5$

The coordinates are (3, 5).

You need to solve the two equations simultaneously to find the coordinates of the point of intersection of the lines.

As y is given as the subject in one of the equations, you could choose to use the method of substitution.

Note: You can also solve simultaneous equations by graphical methods, plotting the graph of each of the equations.

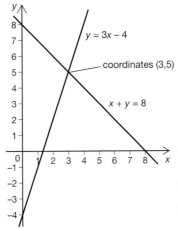

From the graph, the point of intersection is where the equations are solved simultaneously. In this case the point (3, 5) tells us that $x = 3$ and $y = 5$.

Chapter 21 Quadratic equations

Answer	How to solve these questions

Q1 (a) $x^2 + 9x + 14$

(b) $12x^2 - 29x + 14$

(c) $4x^2 - 4x + 1$

Remember to multiply each term in the first bracket by each term in the second bracket.

(c) Remember that $(2x - 1)^2 = (2x - 1)(2x - 1)$.

Q2 (a) $(x + 4)(x - 3)$

(b) $(x - 4)(x + 3)$

(c) Does not factorise.

(c) You can't factorise the quadratic $x^2 + x - 3$.

$x^2 + x - 3 = (x \quad)(x \quad)$

The only numbers that multiply together to give -3 are -3×1 and -1×3.

Neither of these pairs works in the equation.

Q3 (a) $x = 4$ or $x = \frac{7}{2}$ (or $3\frac{1}{2}$)

(b) $x = 3$ or $x = 4$

(c) $x = -\frac{1}{2}$ or $x = 3$

(d) $x = -\frac{1}{2}$ or $x = 3$

(e) $x = 0$ or $x = 10$

(b) $x^2 - 7x + 12 = 0$ is the same as $(x - 3)(x - 4) = 0$.

(c) $2x^2 - 5x - 3 = 0$ is the same as $(2x + 1)(x - 3) = 0$.

(d) $2x^2 - 5x = 3$ can be written as $2x^2 - 5x - 3 = 0$ which is the same as part (c).

(e) You can write $x^2 = 10x$ as $x^2 - 10x = 0$.
Then you can write $x^2 - 10x = 0$ as $x(x - 10) = 0$.

Q4 (a) $(x - 4)(x - 5)$

(b) $x = 0$ or $x = -2$

(b) You can write $x^2 + 2x = 0$ as $x(x + 2) = 0$.

Q5 $a = 5$ and $b = -2$

Multiply out $(3x - 1)(x + 2)$.
$(3x - 1)(x + 2) = 3x^2 + 5x - 2$.
Now compare with $3x^2 + ax + b$.
$a = 5$ and $b = -2$.

Q6 $(a + b)(a - b) = a^2 - b^2$
$1999^2 - 1998^2$
$= (1999 + 1998)(1999 - 1998)$
$= 3997 \times 1$
$= 3997$

Remember that:
$a^2 - b^2 = (a + b)(a - b)$ and
$(a + b)(a - b) = a^2 - b^2$
This is called the **difference of two squares**.

Q7 $32x$

You can use the difference of two squares for this problem, too.
$a^2 - b^2 = (a + b)(a - b)$
so that:
$(x + 8)^2 - (x - 8)^2 = \{(x + 8) + (x - 8)\}\{(x + 8) - (x - 8)\}$
$= \{2x\}\{16\}$
$= 32x$

Q8 **(a)** Area of square $= x \times x = x^2$
Area of triangle $= \frac{1}{2} \times x \times 4$
$\qquad\qquad = 2x$
Total area $= x^2 + 2x$
The area of the shape is $48\,\text{cm}^2$
so:
$x^2 + 2x = 48$

(a)

Area of square $= x \times x = x^2$
Area of triangle $= \frac{1}{2} \times x \times 4 = 2x$
Total area $= x^2 + 2x$
Since the area of the shape is $48\,\text{cm}^2$
$x^2 + 2x = 48$

(b) $x^2 + 2x = 48$
$x^2 + 2x - 48 = 0$
$(x - 6)(x + 8) = 0$
so $x = 6$ or $x = -8$
The length must be positive, so
length $= 6\,\text{cm}$.

(b) Remember that $x^2 + 2x = 48$ is the same as $x^2 + 2x - 48 = 0$.
Solve the quadratic to find $x = 6$ or $x = -8$.
Ignore $x = -8$ as you can't have a negative length.

Answer	**How to solve these questions**

Q1 $y = \dfrac{qx}{x+q}$

Use the flow chart.

> Clear fractions by multiplying both sides by the denominator.

$q(x-y) - xy$

> Multiply out the brackets and rearrange so all the terms that include the subject are on one side.

$qx - qy = xy$
$qx = xy + qy$
$xy + qy = qx$

> Factorise terms containing the subject and divide both sides by the factor.

$y(x+q) = qx$
$y = \dfrac{qx}{x+q}$

Q2 (a) $\dfrac{4}{5}$

(a) $s = \dfrac{1 - (\frac{1}{3})^2}{1 + (\frac{1}{3})^2} = \dfrac{\frac{8}{9}}{\frac{10}{9}}$

$= \dfrac{8}{10} = \dfrac{4}{5}$

(b) $t = \sqrt{\dfrac{1-s}{1+s}}$

(b) Use the flow chart.

> Take out the fractions by multiplying both sides by the denominator.

$s(1 + t^2) = 1 - t^2$

> Multiply out the brackets and rearrange so all the terms that include the subject are on one side.

$s + st^2 = 1 - t^2$
$st^2 + t^2 = 1 - s$

> Factorise terms containing the subject and divide both sides by the factor.

$t^2(s+1) = 1 - s$
$t^2 = \dfrac{1-s}{1+s}$
$t = \sqrt{\dfrac{1-s}{1+s}}$

Q3 $s = \dfrac{p^2 t}{p^2 - 1}$

$p = \sqrt{\dfrac{s}{s-t}}$

$p^2 = \dfrac{s}{s-t}$ (squaring both sides)

Now rearrange the equation, take out s and find the new expression.

Q4 $\dfrac{7x + 21}{2x^2 + 5x - 3}$

$= \dfrac{7\cancel{(x+3)}^1}{(2x-1)\cancel{(x+3)}^1}$

$= \dfrac{7}{2x-1}$

You can always answer these questions in exactly the same way, by factorising (where possible) the numerator and denominator and then cancelling.

Q5 $(x-b)^2 = x^2 - 2bx + b^2$

so $-2b = -10$ or $b = 5$.

$14 + a = b^2$

So $a = 11$ and $b = 5$.

Work out the two expressions and then compare coefficients of x^2, x and the constants.

$x^2 - 2bx + b^2 = x^2 - 10x + 14 + a$
So $-2b = -10$ giving $b = 5$.
Also, $14 + a = b^2$ giving $14 + a = 5^2$
$14 + a = 25$
$a = 11$

Q6 $\dfrac{1}{x-2}+\dfrac{1}{x+3}$

$$=\dfrac{1(x+3)}{(x-2)(x+3)}+\dfrac{1(x-2)}{(x-2)(x+3)}$$

$$=\dfrac{(x+3)+(x-2)}{(x-2)(x+3)}$$

$$=\dfrac{2x+1}{(x-2)(x+3)}$$

You need to start by writing $\dfrac{1}{x-2}+\dfrac{1}{x+3}$ as a single fraction.

Set both terms over a common denominator of $(x-2)(x+3)$ by forming equivalent fractions.

$$\dfrac{1}{x-2}=\dfrac{1(x+3)}{(x-2)(x+3)}$$

$$\dfrac{1}{x+3}=\dfrac{1(x-2)}{(x-2)(x+3)}$$

Now you just need to add the expressions and simplify the numerator.

Q7 $\dfrac{3\times7(2x-3)}{7(x+2)(2x-3)}-\dfrac{2\times7(x+2)}{7(x+2)(2x-3)}$

$$=\dfrac{(x+2)(2x-3)}{7(x+2)(2x-3)}$$

$$\dfrac{21(2x-3)}{7(x+2)(2x-3)}-\dfrac{14(x+2)}{7(x+2)(2x-3)}$$

$$=\dfrac{(x+2)(2x-3)}{7(x+2)(2x-3)}$$

$$\dfrac{42x-63}{7(x+2)(2x-3)}-\dfrac{14x+28}{7(x+2)(2x-3)}$$

$$=\dfrac{2x^2+x-6}{7(x+2)(2x-3)}$$

$$(42x-63)-(14x+28)=2x^2+x-6$$

$$2x^2-27x+85=0$$

$$(2x-17)(x-5)=0$$

$$\text{so } x=\tfrac{17}{2} \text{ or } x=5$$

First, you need to rewrite each term, setting it over a common denominator of $7(x+2)(2x-3)$.

Multiply out the brackets.

Then multiply throughout by $7(x+2)(2x-3)$ to remove the fraction.
Use brackets to keep terms together, before simplifying.
Simplify the resulting expression. You should find it reduces to a quadratic.
Factorise the quadratic.
Solve to find the value of x.

Chapter 23 Further quadratic equations

Q1 $(2x-1)(x+4)$

You can rewrite $2x^2+7x=4$ as $2x^2+7x-4=0$.
Then you can factorise it, in the usual way.

Q2 $x=0$ or $x=\tfrac{2}{3}$

You can factorise the equation $3x^2-2x=0$ as
$x(3x-2)=0$.
You will probably find that this is easier than trying to apply the formula.

Q3 $\dfrac{2}{x+2} = \dfrac{x-1}{x}$

$\dfrac{2x}{x+2} = x-1$

$2x = (x-1)(x+2)$

$2x = x^2 + x - 2$

$x^2 - x - 2 = 0$

$(x-2)(x+1) = 0$

so $x = 2$ or $x = -1$

You can remove the fractions by multiplying both sides of the equation by x, then by $x + 2$.

Then you can multiply out the brackets.

Collect like terms on the same side, and form a quadratic.

You should be able to factorise the quadratic and solve it.

Note: Read Chapter 22 *Further manipulation of equations*, if you need more practice with algebraic fractions.

Q4 $x^2 + 4x - 9 = [(x+2)^2 - 4] - 9$
$\qquad\qquad\quad = (x+2)^2 - 13$

$x^2 + 4x - 9 = 0$

$\Rightarrow (x+2)^2 - 13 = 0$

$\Rightarrow (x+2)^2 = 13$

$\Rightarrow (x+2)^2 = \pm\sqrt{13}$

$\Rightarrow x = -2 \pm \sqrt{13}$

As $(x+2)^2 = x^2 + 4x + 4$
Then $(x+2)^2 - 4 = x^2 + 4x$ or $x^2 + 4x = (x+2)^2 - 4$

From above.

Add 13 to both sides.

Take the square root on both sides and remember both positive and negative roots.

Subtract 2 from both sides.

Q5 For $x^2 - 2x - 1 = 0$
$a = 1, b = -2, c = -1$

Substituting in the formula:

$x = \dfrac{-b \pm \sqrt{b^2 - 4ac}}{2a}$

$x = \dfrac{-(-2) \pm \sqrt{(-2)^2 - 4 \times 1 \times -1}}{2 \times 1}$

$x = \dfrac{+2 \pm \sqrt{4 + 4}}{2}$

$x = \dfrac{2 \pm \sqrt{8}}{2}$

$x = \dfrac{2 + \sqrt{8}}{2}$ or $x = \dfrac{2 - \sqrt{8}}{2}$

$x = 2.414\,213\,562$
$x = 2.41$ (2 d.p.)

$x = -0.414\,213\,562$
$x = -0.41$ (2 d.p.)

Substitute in the formula.

Remember $-(-2) = +2$.

This simplifies to $x = 1 + \dfrac{\sqrt{8}}{2}$ or $x = 1 - \dfrac{\sqrt{8}}{2}$

$\qquad$ or $x = 1 + \sqrt{2}$ or $x = 1 - \sqrt{2}$

$\qquad$ as $\dfrac{\sqrt{8}}{2} = \dfrac{\sqrt{4 \times 2}}{2} = \dfrac{2\sqrt{2}}{2} = \sqrt{2}$.

Q6 (a) $(3x+4)(x-2)$

(b) $x = -\frac{4}{3}$ and $x = 2$

(c) $-1, 0, 1, 2$

(a) You should be able to factorise the quadratic quite easily.

(b) Solve the equation by setting each factor equal to 0.

(c) The values $x = -\frac{4}{3}$ and $x = 2$ divide the number line into three distinct sections i.e. $x < -\frac{4}{3}, -\frac{4}{3} < x < 2$ and $x > 2$.

You can find the answer by testing integer values in these regions.

If you prefer, you could draw a graph, like this.

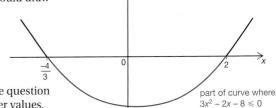

Remember that the question only asks for integer values.

part of curve where $3x^2 - 2x - 8 \leqslant 0$

Published by HarperCollins*Publishers* Limited
77–85 Fulham Palace Road
Hammersmith
London W6 8JB

www.**Collins**Education.com
On-line support for schools and colleges

© HarperCollins*Publishers* Limited 2003

First published 2001
This revised edition published 2004

ISBN 0 00 717093 9

British Library Cataloguing in Publication Data
A catalogue record for this book is available from the British Library

Edited by Joan Miller
Production by Kathryn Botterill
Book design by Gecko Limited
Printed and bound in Hong Kong by Printing Express Ltd.

Acknowledgements
The Author and Publishers are grateful to the following for permission to reproduce copyright material:
AQA/NEAB The following questions: p.9 Q2, p.11 Q5, p.12 Q1, p.27 Q2, p.36 Q1, p.42 Q1, p.50 Q5, p.72 Q3, p.86 Q2, p.88 Q5 are reproduced with the permission of the Assessment and Qualifications Alliance.
AQA/SEG The following questions: p.5 Q1, p.14 Q3, p.22 Q2, p.22 Q5, p.26 Q3, p.33 Q1, p.35 Q4, p.35 Q5, p.38 Q2, p.41 Q2, p.41 Q5, p.49 Q2, p.49 Q3, p.53 Q3, p.55 Q2, p.57 Q2, p.58 Q4, p.58 Q5, p.63 Q2, p.70 Q2, p.72 Q2, p.75 Q3, p.79 Q1, p.85 Q4, p.85 Q5 are reproduced with the permission of the Assessment and Qualifications Alliance.
CCEA The following questions: p.14 Q1, p.35 Q1, p.54 Q4, p.55 Q1, p.68 Q5, p.75 Q5 are reproduced with the permission of the Northern Ireland Council for the Curriculum Examinations.
Edexcel The following questions: p.32 Q2, p.49 Q1, p.33 Q2, p.18 Q4, p.59 Q7, p.75 Q4 are reproduced with the permission of Edexcel.
OCR The following questions: p.5 Q2, p.7 Q1, p.7 Q3, p.11 Q4, p.16 Q2, p.23 Q2, p.29 Q1, p.32 Q3, p.39 Q2, p.44 Q4, p.50 Q4, p.50 Q7, p.51 Q1, p.57 Q1, p.57 Q3, p.59 Q6, p.63 Q1, p.64 Q4, p.69 Q1, p.72 Q4, p.75 Q1, p.75 Q6, p.81 Q4, p.88 Q2, p.88 Q3 are reproduced with the permission of Oxford Cambridge RSA Examinations.
WJEC The following questions: p.11 Q1, p.15 Q1, p.18 Q5, p.22 Q4, p.12 Q2, p.23 Q1, p.26 Q2, p.29 Q3, p.32 Q1, p.35 Q6, p.60 Q1, p.65 Q5, p.68 Q2, p.73 Q2, p.75 Q2, p.81 Q8, p.82 Q1, p.85 Q7, p.86 Q1, are reproduced with the permission of the Welsh Joint Education Committee/Cyd-bwyllgor Addysg Cymru.
Note: The Awarding Bodies listed above accept no responsibility whatsoever for the accuracy or method of working in the answers given, which are solely the responsibility of the author and publishers.

Illustrations
Cartoon Artwork – Dave Mostyn

Every effort has been made to contact the holders of copyright material, but if any have been inadvertently overlooked, the Publishers will be pleased to make the necessary arrangements at the first opportunity.

You might also like to visit:
www.**fire**and**water**.com
The book lover's website